T0149573

SABOTAGE

SABOTAGE

EXPOSING THE SATANIC SABOTAGE
SET AGAINST EVERY GOD-INSPIRED
DREAM, VISION, PURPOSE, AND
DESTINY WITHIN YOUR LIFE

KEVIN A. JOHNSON

authorHOUSE®

AuthorHouse™
1663 Liberty Drive
Bloomington, IN 47403
www.authorhouse.com
Phone: 1-800-839-8640

Cover illustration by LeAnna Massingille
Cover and page design by LeAnna Massingille

Published by AuthorHouse   03/14/2012

ISBN: 978-1-4685-6323-8 (sc)
ISBN: 978-1-4685-6322-1 (hc)
ISBN: 978-1-4685-6321-4 (e)

Library of Congress Control Number: 2012905047

Any people depicted in stock imagery provided by Thinkstock are models, and such images are being used for illustrative purposes only.
Certain stock imagery © Thinkstock.

This book is printed on acid-free paper.

I wish to dedicate this book to the awesome Savior of the world, Jesus Christ. It is He alone who supplied the vision and insight for every page of this book. He has not just given to us, His church, the ability to see the sabotage of Satan, but He has given his whole life to insure that every human being on this planet can find peace with God and escape from the dominion of Satan. I also wish to dedicate this book to all of you who will read this written documentation of God's great escape. It is my sincere desire that you will know Jesus and walk in His light, so that you will be able to escape every satanic trap set against your life.

CONTENTS

Preface
ix

One
Enemy of the God Design
1

Two
Born with the Sabotage Gene
11

Three
Dangerous Words
15

Four
Killer Thoughts
25

Five
The Mind of the Defeated
37

Six

Unseen Things: The Most Dangerous
Things to a God-Destined Life
62

Seven

The Bigger the Giant, the Greater the Destiny
79

Eight

Surviving the Lion's Den: Your Exit Strategy
97

About The Author
107

PREFACE

SAVED, SANCTIFIED, AND moving with God's power in the Holy Ghost, you sleep. You move effortlessly by the awesome grace of God, through the deep darkness of this satanic world order, without so much as a flesh wound of the enemy. You seem to have arrived at a beautiful and tranquil place in God-a state of mind in which you feel untouchable. Everything you touch in your life turns to gold and every vision that God has for your life is unfolding and manifesting right on schedule. You are invincible. You constantly remind yourself that nothing can go wrong. You gaze into the deep future with eyes filled with God's holy light as you shout the words of faith: "I shall never be moved!" The future then seems to cry out to you in that very moment: "You will possess all that is in me!"

While you are at such a place of purposeful rest, a place where nothing within your world can ever go wrong, you hear a knock on the door of God's creative destiny for your life. This knock is like none you have ever heard. The sound is penetrating to your soul, and all of a sudden you feel a cold and migrating chill come across your entire body. You shout out from the state of terror that wants to take your very voice, "Who is it!?" You drop every thought of greatness and future conquests as you would a drinking glass, as you realize that what is knocking on your life's door is not a "who" but a "what." Just when all seems to be going right and the Lord has shone His wonderful light upon your existence, a dark and menacing cloud hangs over your doorpost. A voice shakes you to the very core of your being as if it were the sound of a thousand bellowing bells: "I am Sabotage!"

While finally catching your last breath and finding yourself in the uncharted waters of this very inescapable reality, you ask the million dollar question: "What do you want with me?"

In this gut-wrenching and heart-pounding moment, the spirit of sabotage informs you that it is a part of your God-led destiny and has come to challenge every God-laid and God-designed vision, dream, and purpose for your life. You realize in this moment that you must face this giant.

I believe, as God's Spirit-led author of this book, that many Christians are finding themselves in this unfamiliar place at this very precious moment in their walk with God. You must understand that whenever and wherever God chooses to move, there will always be demonic and satanic-orchestrated plans designed to sabotage God's wonderful and life-saving agenda. Even in the New Testament Book of Matthew 13:24-30, Jesus shares a parable explaining that as soon as the kingdom seed of God is sown, enemies immediately sow tares (seeds of distraction and sabotage) into the very field containing God's dreams and purposes for every soul's life. This parable is a warning to every child of God to always be alert and watchful in prayer because Satan is on the move. Satan's objective is to defeat you and God's plan for your life by setting up traps that are hard for you to recognize. You must be aware that Satan does not go for the kill right away. Instead, he takes small, bite-size chunks out of our dreams and God's destiny for us until he has devoured our entire God-breathed lives.

Sabotage is a spirit that you and I can never truly escape until Jesus returns to rapture us off of this planet. As we walk through this life, seeking God and desiring to manifest His love-life to sinful and dying people, we will, from moment to moment, find ourselves in its presence. Please realize that every great vessel of faith in the Bible had to face this nemesis. Adam and Eve, who birthed the entire human race, faced the first sabotage strike in world history. Then there was Abel, a son of Adam, in whose day people began to call on God once more. Well, he was killed by his brother Cain because Satan did not want people to seek and find the reality of God on the earth again. Let's not forget David. When Saul, who had invited David to the palace to play an instrument and quiet his soul, discovered that David would replace him as king, he attempted to kill David on more than one occasion. Saul was attempting to sabotage David's God- appointed place on the throne as king of Israel. Now, if these men had to endure sabotage, what does this tell you?

The greater the anointing and calling of God on any one of His vessels, the greater the size, shape, and magnitude of the satanic sabotage set for this individual. Satan has planned sabotage from the womb. In today's world, even before babies are born and their purpose established, Satan has ensured that abortion would be the reality for millions of them. Abortion for the purpose of simply getting rid of an unwanted conception is one of the most destructive and deadliest tools of sabotage in Satan's toolbox. This kind of genocide (the willful termination and murder of millions of human lives) seeks to kill the child before it can even live outside the womb and live unto God. Satan knows that the best way to eliminate the will of God on this earth is to cut out every potential human vessel God wishes to use to accom plish His agenda and purpose for mankind. Therefore, Satan figures that if he kills them before God can truly use them, then God would have no vessels among men to birth his plans on the earth. Satan tried the same thing around the time of the birth of Jesus. He influenced the mind of Herod and had him kill every male infant up to the age of two in an effort to kill the potential King of the prophecy and prevent Him from taking his place. Now one must understand that Satan was trying to kill God's Messiah before He arrived at the place of the cross, God's sacrificial destiny for him. Jesus needed to make it to the cross so that His earthly death was in complete harmony with God's heavenly prophecy.

But Satan realizes that the sabotage of abortion alone is not enough, and so he sets up traps in the lives of the children that he hopes will either kill them or prevent them from walking in God's divine destiny. One of the traps occurs when children reach adolescence and begin to experience strong emotional and sensual feelings. It is at this time that Satan plans that first sexual and wrong encounter for their lives. Many young people, at this moment of satanic distraction and deception, have either caught AIDS or another STD, or may have caused a pregnancy. Therefore, instead of that precious child preparing for sports, college, or marriage, it is possible that he or she will spend much of life dealing with the consequences of his or her wreckless actions. Thus, before this child has even begun to live, he or she must already prepare for health problems or perhaps even death. Additionally, the child that becomes pregnant is also sabotaged because before this child can even plan or think about any kind of future for herself, she must now make plans for two. This child has to focus on another life's needs before she can focus on her own. Many young people have thrown away a large portion of their existence before they have even learned the importance of it.

The seeds of sabotage are everywhere. Just like a plague of killer bees, sabotage is lurking, growing, and swarming- taking lives by the millions. Many great minds will never have a chance to reveal their brilliance to the inhabitants of this earth because in some school or at some park or in some drug- infested neighborhood, they are taking their first smoke of a marijuana joint or their first hit of cocaine. For some, the sabotage of choice is found at the bottom of thousands of emptied beer or liquor bottles. Many are content to simply drink away their futures and their God-given potential. In this generation, so many people have died or become injured due to some careless and callous drunk driver. Many potentially great lives and destined human beings have been killed not because they abused alcohol, but because someone else did. What a waste of potential and an awful rape of innocent life.

The longer one lives, one cannot help but see the trees that the seeds of sabotage have reproduced. One case in point is the young boy or girl who is sexually molested as a child. Later, as an adult, this same person is now caught sexu ally molesting another child. Therefore, the cycle of sexual abuse continues. Satan planned to destroy this life not in its adult stage, but in its innocent childhood stage. Thus, the tree, without God's help, is only as good or as evil as its seed. Another case of sabotaging the tree at the seed stage is when an individual is a victim of rape as a child and then rapes someone else as an adult. Sometimes a victim's sabotaged life becomes a predator's life, filled with rage and abusive tendencies. Through this means of operation, Satan can get one sabotaged life to sabotage millions more.

After coming into this kind of God-breathed and inspired revelation, it is vital to ensure that your life is led, empowered, and influenced completely by the Holy Spirit. Like it or not, no matter how deep in God you might be or how anointed you think you are, sabotage will and already has paid you a visit. The seed of sabotage has predated you. Long before you were Spirit reborn, you were born into a family with some secret sins or open failures. Only by obeying the Holy Spirit will you be delivered from sins that trapped others before you. You see, there are some sins within our families that affect us and act as sabotage seeds against us even though we are hidden in Christ. Now, you may not be judged for your father's or mother's sins, but you can be affected by them if you do not ask the Lord to break their generational chains. Once we learn about our family's sin weaknesses, we can take that knowledge into the secret place of prayer and break that stronghold through the twin sisters of fasting and worshipping in the presence of the Holy Ghost. In the same manner that a skilled doctor can only help us by knowing what is wrong with us, we too must recognize the seeds of sabotage in our families and in our personal lives in order for us to be delivered and made whole. So, my friends, do not take for granted the knowledge that alcoholism exists in your family. You must take seriously the vices of addiction in your family, or those *very* addictions may take you out. The sins of one generation, if left unchecked, might become the downfall and brokenness, the sabotaged reality, of the next.

This book has been inspired by the Holy Spirit to help saints and sinners recognize the potentially killer sabotage seeds in this earth. My hope is that you would allow Jesus Christ complete rule within your lives so that He can crush the power of Satan's seeds of sabotage before they become deadly and poisonous fruit trees. I wish, by the power of the Holy Spirit, to let you know that God did not intend for you to live a life under the control of sabotage, and He does not want you to stay in the valley of sabotage but to pass through it. Jesus Christ is that unseen sabotage buffer; He is waiting for you to give yourself completely over to Him so that you can live the life of a conquering victor.

Chapter One

Enemy of the God Design

For every God-made, designed, and purposed thing, there exists a satanic and destructive strategy to sabotage it. Yes, indeed. If God made it or desires to have it, you had better believe that Satan has his crooked eyes set to destroy it, or at least pervert it, and make it his own. You should be aware that there is nothing on this planet which God has marked for His use and purpose that Satan has not already marked for death and destruction. There is always an enemy of the God design. Since this fact is clear, you should spend as much time learning about your enemy, the devil, as you spend learning about your God and His purpose for your very spiritual and physical existence. "Why learn about your enemy?" you might ask. Well, by the Holy Ghost's wisdom, I will tell you. It is vital that you know your enemy and know him well because Satan is targeting you and is coming after every God-inspired vision and dream in your Spirit-birthed life. Therefore, if you cannot recognize him when he shows up, you will not live long enough to even begin, much less end, what God has designed for you. One of the most destructive and dangerous actions in this life is to be looking right at your enemy and talking with him as though he were your friend. People get killed this way!

In the field of police investigation, many criminals get caught because they can be traced. Police officers or investigators can trace the path of many criminals by using either that person's fingerprint or bodily tissue left at the scene. Well, in the same way that a criminal can be traced, so too can Satan and his demons be traced, and you can know if they are or were at work in your life.

Satan might be deceptively smart and careful, but with the eyes of discernment, you can detect him. If you attempt to simply use your physical abilities of seeing, hearing, feeling, tasting, and smelling to try and watch for Satan's movement, you will miss him. The use of these senses is profitable when trying to uncover something in the physical world, but these basic and fragile human abilities are neither sharp enough nor penetrating enough to break through the shadowy world of the satanic or demonic. Therefore, the only way to trace or track something spiritual is by using that which is also spiritual. Thank God He gave us His living and spiritual Word, filled with His decoding and tracking words of life. By much study of the Bible, God's major tool for discerning or uncovering His ways and those of Satan, we can train our natural senses to shut down or shut off, and enable the senses within our spirit to scout out any spiritual terrain and know what demons are at work and how they are operating. This is awesome! Although discernment received from studying the penetrating Word of God is an awesome tool, God also gives the Christian a greater ability to see into the spirit realm through a gift of the Holy Ghost, called the gift of discerning of spirits. With this gift, one could trace the work of demons back for many generations, and could come to understand how many there are and how much damage they have done or intend to inflict. To receive this gift, one must simply seek God and ask Him to release it. Every believer must be able to track the enemy of God's purpose and designs. We must know Satan's plans in advance if we are going to finish or fulfill God's mission and mandate for our lives.

Now that you are well aware that God has provided ways to track Satan's movements, you also need to know how Satan looks when he moves. Please do not believe that the devil is dressed in red cloth, holds a pitchfork in his hand, and has a headgear of two horns. Boy! If only it were that simple to trace him. Actually, you will not be able to detect Satan by what he wears, instead, you will be able to see him by how he acts. Yes, indeed! You will be able to see through any mask he wears or any human face through whom he is working by realizing that Satan's actions will give him away every time.

The first dead giveaway that Satan is at work against you is that he always gets offended in the presence of anything godly. People who are easily offended when you are talking about God and are quick to say, "All right, enough of that God talk now!" or "Why do we always have to talk about God?" are being used by Satan to silence your testimony or scare your witness. The devil gets very uncomfortable when you praise and worship God. Those in your life who never want to join you in praising God or are scared to be known as your friend at work simply because others overhear you praising God at the office are not true friends and could be a vessel of Satan to make you uncomfortable with your praise life. Whenever you take time out from the tedious work day to read the Bible and pray and someone very close to you wants you to go shopping at the mall instead, you had better realize who is operating behind that individual. It is amazing how many times Satan has gotten us up off our knees and to quit praying, influenced us to hide the Bible away for years in neglect, and helped with the total stunting of our spiritual growth simply by using people or things that we did not suspect or expect him to use. We need to wake up! Satan is the enemy of everything that God stands for, and he will not be still and allow us to befriend all that is of God.

The second action that will reveal Satan every time is that he cannot tell the truth. Satan is the daddy of lies. Any thought that comes into your mind that is of Satan will never lead you into an action or end result that is truthful. You see, Satan can never influence you to do anything that is correct. Thus, to determine if any thought or word is a lie from Satan before you act on it, visualize the end result of doing or saying such a thing. If the end result of that word or action would be you or someone else dying, you or someone else getting hurt, someone's name being falsely damaged, or you or someone else walking away from God and into sin, you can know that word or action is from the enemy. How many times do we say, "Oops" because we acted on thoughts or words that we assumed were from God's mouth but were actually from Satan's twisted mouth.

A third action of Satan is that of perversion. When something is perverted, it means that it has been altered from its original intent or purpose. Satan is the master of making a correct thing wrong. He is the great artist at taking a true image and deforming it and its purpose. Satan is always at work when you know God's commands and then see other actions that you know could not be God's will. If God requires a man and a woman to be married before having sex, then Satan will attempt to change this true way. Now, many people believe that since sex is good and God made it, you do not really have to be married; you just need to be in love. Sadly, many Christians have come to accept this as truth. In the church of Jesus Christ, many who have not detected Satan at work have already been tricked into defiling their minds as well as their bodies. Perversion is a seed of sabotage that causes many to become so vile before God's face that God can no longer be among them. In the church of today, there are men who perform perverted sexual acts with other men, and women who perform sexual acts with women. Sadly, many claim that these actions are okay in God's sight; they have been twisted by Satan to believe that if they have these feelings within them and God made them, then God must have made them gay. When people believe that right is wrong and wrong is right and, especially, that the wrong way is somehow a work of God, then everything becomes so confusing that people are no longer able to separate the truth from lies and goodness from wickedness, and Satan wins. Perversion! What a dangerous tool of sabotage! Be very assured that God made man and woman to have sexual relations in the bond and covenant of marriage. This is the unadulterated and untwisted truth!

At this juncture in your reading of this book, you should realize the massive scope of Satan's desire to sabotage every God-planned dream, goal, or strategy for your life. Please also be assured that this saboteur will go to extreme lengths and will stop at nothing to ensure that you die having never accomplished God's will or design for you. You must therefore be very aware of

Satan's fourth method of sabotage-closeness. Yes, indeed! Satan will use anyone or anything that is near and dear to your heart in an attempt to throw you off of your Godstrategized game. In life, one rarely thinks that serious hurt will come from a parent or a close friend. We generally believe that the closer someone is to us, the more they would want to protect and help us. However, as you grow and go through life's experiences, you find out that this is not entirely true; in fact, by this time you may have already been wounded almost to death. Satan will use those closest to us because he knows that we rarely doubt any word they would say to us. Therefore, if a parent says to a child, "You are so stupid!" that child tends to quickly accept this as true, because in that child's mind, the parent could not be wrong. How many times have you been tricked into aborting a dream, goal, prayer, praise, or spiritual growth because a close friend told you that you could not or should not do it. If your answer to this question is "Many times," then you need to have what I call a "friend change." You must realize that the Holy Spirit will never tell you to abort growing in the Lord or tell you that it is impossible for you to finish college or start that business you have been dreaming about. So many people are behind physical prison bars today because they listened to a close friend. So many suicides have occurred because some teenagers believed a satanic and abusive lie from the lips of a parent who knew no better. Damning words such as stupid, dumb, and no good echoed so loudly in their ears that these teenagers became convinced that ending their seemingly pathetic and miserable lives would be doing daddy or mommy a huge favor. Even as adults, we find ourselves hijacked and sabotaged by a close coworker who told us that we could never get that promotion or that we should go ahead and sleep with that coworker since our marriage is falling apart anyway. Many girls have gotten pregnant and dropped out of school all because they believed the satanic lie that having sex will make them feel loved, coming from the mouth of a best friend who maybe has never had sex either. Many teenagers have contracted diseases during their first sexual encounter simply because close friends dared them to have sex with a complete stranger. Now, many hospital or clinic visits later, these same teenagers are suffering and have been rejected by the same close friends who encouraged them to have sex in the first place. Satan has tapped into the powerful resource of using closeness as his major killer of destiny, plans, goals, dreams, and passion for God. In essence, Satan has found a way for us to kill ourselves, sometimes without our even knowing it. What a master plan!

Surely you do not think that these four previously mentioned actions of sabotage are the only weapons in Satan's arsenal. No way! And not by a long shot! Satan, the enemy of the God design, often deploys weapon number five, and it is the believe-what-you-see vision. Satan knows that if he can control a person's vision, he can damage or defeat that person's life. Oh, yes! Vision is of utmost importance. Satan intends to persuade people that their lives are only as real as what they see. Therefore, if I visualize long enough that I was born in poverty, soon I will begin to act poor, live poor, and feel so defeated by my poverty that I might just die poor. Millions of Christians around the globe today are living defeated and faithless lives because they have allowed Satan to dictate what they can afford, what they can accomplish, or how far they can climb on the ladder of success by placing before them a visionary buffet of all the negative aspects of their lives. Therefore, if they see that they are poor, they automatically believe that they can never be rich. If they recognize that they are weak, they believe that they can never be strong. Some believe that they will always be an alcoholic because all that they have known within their family is alcoholism. People tend to believe exactly what they see, and unless the power of God's Spirit changes their twisted vision, they will usually live defeated because of what they have seen. Satan has been setting up the props in plain sight, but people have been readily accepting those props as the only true reality in their lives. Thus, it is not just the crimes of robbery, rape, or murder that places people behind prison bars; it is the deep, dark satanic vision that causes them to believe that all they will ever be in life are thieves, rapists, or murderers. Oh, yes! People usually believe only what they see. This sighted life stems all the way back to Adam and Eve's decision to live by sight by eating from a tree of the wrong sight, in order to become sighted like God. Well, they made a very dangerous mistake. You see, after eating the fruit from the tree, another kind of sight was opened to them. At first they walked by faith and the vision of God, but by eating from the tree of the knowledge of good and evil, they had confined themselves to a knowledge based upon what they could see right in front of them or around them. Thus, they passed on this very dangerous and imperfect way of living to us, and only Jesus Christ has the power and spiritually true vision to replace our false and deceptive one. However, this reality does not stop Satan from tempting us to live by what we see. In fact, many Christians are walking away from holy living and God's purpose because their spiritual and living sight has been contaminated by the deceptive, enticing, and beautiful outward appearance of worldly things. Many have given their vision over to lusting after cars, houses, megachurches, or great reputations. Satan has caught them in deadly traps by their own lustful and pleasure-filled visions. Now, all they want is that extramarital affair and not the true vision of the true wife which God has given them. This is why many Christian marriages are falling to the earth and breaking into pieces. Too many Christian spouses believe that the vision of the spouse they have now is not enough, so they have gone over to the other side where the grass looks greener. Then, after losing the best thing in their lives, they realize that the grass they thought was so green on the other side was actually AstroTurf and not even real grass. How many lives or marriages have to die before we realize that we should never place our trust in only what we see? This is why the Bible admonishes us to walk by faith. Faith gives us the truest sight of what is really happening to us and reveals why. Faith is the God view which lets us know that although we were born in sin, we are made righteous through Jesus Christ. Faith lets us know that although we look frail and weak, in God we are really strong and mighty. It also allows us to see that although our parents birthed us in poverty, we have been reborn by the Holy Ghost into a very rich kingdom.

Hey, it is time for us to rise up in the power of God and let the enemy know that, by the divine revelation of God's Spirit, we can now see him coming. When you are able to recognize Satan every time he comes at you or sends one of his demonic slaves after you, his job becomes much more difficult because you can be victorious over him every time. I encourage you to keep seeking God, keep recognizing the enemy of the God design, and avoid every destiny trap of Satan.

CHAPTER TWO

BORN WITH THE SABOTAGE GENE

IN ANOTHER CASE, some women are always searching for a man to fulfill them because they witnessed their mothers looking for the same fulfillment. In the church today, there are so many Christian women getting into relationships with men, thinking that this will make them whole. Sadly, they fall into the same trap as their mothers and end up brokenhearted, single, and parenting a child or children alone. It may seem amazing in each of these cases that children do not learn from the mistakes of their parents. Instead, they have actually perfected these imperfections and gained the same results, or worse. In fact, they have increased the effects of these failures, and, if they do not repent, they will pass on the same errant mindset to their sons and daughters.

It is vital for us to know the burdensome baggage we are carrying around in our flesh. Now, we had no choice concerning through whom we would be born or what sins would be passed onto us. However, by the power of Jesus Christ, we can be transformed from this sabotage gene and live according to a new and eternal genetic code, the Spirit gene. While we are learning to walk in the spirit of this new and radical gene, we must be aware that the sabotage gene will not go away quietly or just remain dead. This old gene system will fight us to the very end.

One of the hardest realities to face is that we often fail because of what is within us rather than what is around us.

This is a very frustrating experience. There are occasions when it seems as though we are going to get that promotion, only to discover that we lost it because we gossiped too much about our fellow colleagues. Thus, the inner sabotage gene of gossip, which happened to be passed down from our mothers and was deemed cute, has just cost us the job we have been waiting on for years. Or, how about going to the doctor and discovering that the cancer from which your father died is now in your lungs because, like your father before you, you just had to take up the "art" of cigarette smoking. Now, your life and destiny have been cut short, and the pain of your father's struggle with lung cancer is now yours.

Consider this hypothetical situation. Here is a young man who happens to be the heavy favorite to win a basketball scholarship to Duke University. Shortly after leading his high school team to the coveted national championship, he is well on his way to Duke. Can you just for a moment picture him? He is excited! His whole life ahead of him and a future stake in the NBA awaits him. News reporters are already salivating over the prospect of being the first to write of his nearly assured NBA career. Do you see him in your mind's eye? He is happy, isn't he? Then, picture him at the university. Things are going well. He stumbles around, managing to find his way to every class. It's the happiest season of his young, potential-filled life. However, after being in school for several weeks, he becomes overwhelmed by the work load and practice schedule. One day, a young man approaches him. Taking hold of his jacket, he rushes him into a nearby bathroom. While he ponders the meaning of this, the young man slips two pills into his pocket and tells him that these pills will help him get through the demanding times and days on the university's campus. Without hesitation, he takes the pills out of his pocket and immediately takes them. Suddenly, his mind starts to wander off and his heart beats so rapidly that it feels as if he is about to fly. He then falls to the ground, clutching his chest, and dies instantly. Later that day, his cold, stiff body is discovered by one of his teammates.

After the police have finished their preliminary investigation at the scene of this horrific accident, his body is taken for an autopsy. Soon, an autopsy report is given to the boy's brokenhearted and confused parents, and it leaves them in complete shock. The report explains that the young man, who had never taken any kind of legal or illegal drug in his entire life, died of a drug overdose. While the parents are weeping because of the immense pain over the loss of their son, they begin to reflect on how their son's uncle, Jim, had died. You see, Uncle Jim died due to a cocaine overdose two years prior to his nephew's death. It appears that he had begun to tell his nephew about the awesome experience of drugs, placing the deadly seed thoughts into the mind of this impressionable young man. This drove him to be so curious about the heavenly bliss associated with drugs that it made him an easy target for any drug dealer. Now this boy, just like his uncle before him, got an itch for trying drugs and needed to scratch that itch so badly that it cost him his life and killed his God-breathed potential. I believe that if we were to search long enough, we would discover millions of sad stories like this one.

We must consider the evidence that even when we are born of the Holy Ghost and covered in the righteousness of God, we still struggle with the flesh. This truth should make us *very* sensitive to and very watchful over what we allow ourselves to see and think. If we are not careful in this, we might find that the sabotage gene within our fleshy desires and old way of thinking resurrects and causes the death of God's vision in us. Whether we like it or not, as long as we follow after the things of God, there lives a monster sabotage gene deep within our subconscious mind. This gene strives to come alive in our conscious thoughts in order to reign in and over our natural human bodies for the expressed purpose of drowning out the voice of God's Spirit within us. We must realize that this is one diabolical and sinfully disturbed genie that we do not want to let out of its lamp.

CHAPTER THREE

DANGEROUS WORDS

WRONG WORDS ARE like hard stones-they can break the bones of God's agenda, vision, and purpose for your life. Present dangerous words, if allowed, can hurt future productivity!

Have you ever had big plans for your life? Have you spent every waking day and sleepless night working on and preparing for just the right moment to begin them, only to have your intense passion come crashing down due to one stupid word from a supposedly wise friend? That one satanic and well-placed word seemed to take all of the air out of your purpose balloon. Oh, yes! There are some words that, if allowed, can hijack every God-ordained plan for your life.

You see, Satan knows that the best means of destroying God's agenda in your life is not by throwing physical stones at it but by throwing discouraging, word-like stones into your very fragile mind. He knows the power of words. After all, he witnessed God create the heavens and the earth by the power of His words. Satan also knows that God rules by His words. Therefore, Satan understands that by using persuasive and negative words, instead of physical weapons, he can get us to kill our own God-appointed destiny without him having to lift a finger. By feeding our minds with dangerous words, he intends to have our own minds become our worst enemies.

Words are powerful and have a way of awakening specific appetites in our human bodies and minds. For example, if I were to say the words, "peanut butter," you would think about eating food. Therefore, my injecting these words into your mind causes your appetite for food to speak and your craving for food could become intense. Thus, it is most important that we be very careful about the words we allow into our impressionable minds. The words we hear help form the words we will speak, and the words will eventually be instrumental in shaping the lives we live. So, if we spend too much time listening to negative words, we Will end up very negative people, and we will make our entire life a negative space. Words can either sabotage our future or establish our destiny.

There are dangerous words in this earth, and, regardless of where we live, there are people being used by Satan as sabotage agents. In life, never believe everything that you hear and, most important, never listen to everything that is spoken. Every dream, vision, or calling of God has that one specific, dangerous word intended to destroy it. Satan is seeking to defeat your destiny, and you had better believe that his weapon of choice is dangerous words.

Words are such an awesome weapon that the wrong words can incite a war and the right words can bring about a great peace. The very instant you begin your journey with God, filled with heavenly light, joy, and passion, Satan sends two of the most dangerous words that you will probably every hear. He utters the words, "Just like." Thus, every time you attempt to grow in the knowledge of God, Satan reminds you that it is all a waste of time because you will never change and that you will be "just like" your father or mother. As you attempt to live a life above the failure of your father's adulterous life, in the back of your mind Satan reminds you that you will fail just like him. Maybe you are running away from the great alcoholism monster that has plagued generations of women in your family. Until this time, by God's grace, you have been good at dodging every bar and club, but in your mind, you keep battling the screaming words telling you that you are going to be an alcoholic just like others in your family.

Maybe by God's grace you have overcome the dangerous words "just like." You must still be very aware that Satan has been a saboteur for a long time, and he has many more dangerous words to throw around. There are two other words Satan uses in order to hide you from God's wonderful beauty for your life. These two words happen to be "See how." God informs you by prophetic utterance that you are going to be a millionaire and bless others and Satan immediately comes along and tells you, "See how poor you are!" Suddenly, you decide that it will never happen and then you begin to admit with your own mouth that it could never happen. So, you end up right where you started-poor and miserable-because you allowed your ignorant mind to cash Satan's doubt check.

God has given you awesome health. Then, one day while visiting the doctor, you get a report that you have cancer. In one minute you have emotionally gone from a mountain-top high to a gut-wrenching valley. The next thing you hear in your ear is the sweet melodious voice of God telling you that you are healed and that you will be fine. As you begin to explode with excitement, Satan steps in with his dangerous words: "See how." He echoes, "See how sick you are!" You then begin to reflect on the doctor's report instead of God's report. You soon realize that you are becoming more ill instead of getting better. It is amazing how words can either heal or bring sickness or even death. Truly, there are some very dangerous words in this life, and, if we are not careful to shut them out of our minds, we will be destined to die by them.

Perhaps you are a person called and chosen by God to bring millions of lost souls into God's kingdom. God has anointed you with a rare calling and placed His awesome power of evangelistic persuasion on your lips. However, just as God sends the season for the fulfillment of this calling, Satan sings a word into your soul: "Remember." With this word, Satan wants you to remember your sinful past. He tempts you to think that God can never truly use your life because you were once a thief, murderer, or something else horrific. By getting you to remember, Satan is causing you to throw away the beauty of your future by reflecting too much on the ugliness of your past. Many people on this earth will never have a God-filled future because they are too busy remem bering and focusing on a God-less past. Therefore, the word "remember" may seem harmless, but can be a very dangerous word. Be very assured that when God wants you to remember anything from your past, it is only to cause you to reflect on how far He has brought you. It is Satan who wants you to disbelieve God's future plans for your life. It is fascinating how this one word, depending on which spirit being is using it, can invoke two entirely different feelings and experiences.

As if the words which you have read about so far weren't bad enough, the word "comfortable" also takes its place among them. On the surface, this word seems harmless. It is a word you could get used to hearing or even using. But I tell you, this word is an accident waiting to happen. Many people will never make it beyond high school because they are comfortable with just having a high school diploma. Many will never grow deeper in God because they are comfortable where they are in their relationship with Him. Many athletes will never set a world or Olympic record simply because they are comfortable with the time or height which they are able to achieve. By this word, potential is stunted and growth is stilled. The world around us did not develop and become this booming connectivity of industry, commerce, and science by people being comfortable. Nations have become industrial and scientific giants by encouraging citizens to be constantly developing and discovering. New worlds in space and on earth would not have been discovered if only comfortable people, and not pioneering adventurers, existed. Think about it! If the physical world of sinful mankind requires people who are not still, lazy, or comfortable in order to thrive and increase, what do you think about God's kingdom? God's kingdom also demands that its citizens be productive, passionate, and in spiritual motion. God has no use for believers who have grown comfortable just serving God at 10 percent and never pushing for 100 percent in their service unto God. Satan knows that one of the fastest ways to kill a race of people or the God-birthed potential within them is to get them comfortable right where they are in life or in God. If he can persuade them to believe that they don't need to accomplish more for God or learn more of God, then they would stop moving forward, growing deeper, and searching for more of God. Thus, they would eventually dry up and die. Never get too comfortable with your job, church, growth level, or life. There is so much more that you can be doing and becoming for God in each of these experiences.

Another dangerous word which you need to filter out of your life, if you have already innocently allowed it in, is "never." With this word, Satan is quick to point out to you that someone else will get that job but never you. Healing does exist, but you will never be healed. The devil is quick to show you a future that could be very real, but then he will inform you that you will never live out that future. So many have come to accept this word in their lives that they have stopped trying anything. More potential new businesses never made it from the visionary's drawing board because they were told it would never happen. Think about how many students have dropped out of school after being told they would never graduate. For every, "Yes, I can" slogan, there is a "Never will" advertisement campaign. Many ministries have died because some people who were called by God to help or sow finances into them never did. You must believe completely in what God is telling you to do and have the resolve to go after it wholeheartedly because your critics will never believe for you. Whether you like it or not, you will hear the word "never" on the job, at school, in church, and even in your own home. It is up to you to ignore it and keep on believing. If you stop believing, then the word "never" will have won and you will, in fact, never become all that God has made you to become.

For those of you reading this book who are married, you should know that there is one word that must be avoided or both you and your spouse will end up broken and the marriage left in utter chaos. In fact, one of the reasons marriages fail is because of this one word. This dangerous word that I am writing about is "better." Many husbands are no longer attracted to their wives, nor wives to their husbands, because they believe that after twenty or fifty years of marriage, they can do better. There are husbands and wives who find themselves gazing at the grass on the other side of the marital fence because they believe they could have done better. Sometimes, and in some cases, the word "better" is truly a good and productive word. However, in the context of a marriage where a spouse believes that he or she can do better, it is a dangerous word. Some husbands have even gone to the extreme of either killing or having their wives killed, and some wives have gone to this same extreme because they wanted to find, or thought that they had found, a better lover. When you are in a struggling marriage, trying to get to the surface in order to catch a breath of fresh oxygen, things always look better on the outside of that marriage. It is human nature to want to escape to another place or into the arms of a better lover. However, if God has not given you freedom to search for better, and the Word of God has not released you from your marriage, then there is still good reason to stand in God's power and allow Him to either remake your spouse or remake you, or both. Before you attempt to make a break for something better, you should fast and pray for God to perform a supernatural remake of your marriage. God can indeed make better a spouse that, in your eyes, has no chance of becoming better. Many great marriages have self-destructed and families have been left in broken pieces, sabotaged by the dangerous word "better." Please do not allow yours to fall into this statistical category!

While I was growing up in the Bahamas, on the island of New Providence, I was hit hard with words that would constantly tempt me to doubt my value, question my reason for being, and shut up the awesome potential of God for my life. I was born very poor, but I had a mother who fought hard to give my brother, sister, and me a normal and good life. Although she tried to do the very best with the cards life had dealt her, she could not rescue me from the mud fight that Satan had planned for me. I can still remember those terrifying words sent by Satan to steal and kill the God-given worth within my life, as if they had just been spoken. The words "You are nothing!" rang in my ears like one thousand bells, dragging me down with every loud and noisome ring. While in school, I could hear these words so loudly that I fell from a B-student to just barely making Ds. I started to purposely miss classes at school because I had given up trying to become anything. Since I believed that I was nothing, I began to act and talk like I was nothing until, eventually, no one could convince me that I had any value or worth. This was one of the worst times in my life! Oh, boy! I was so depressed that I tried just about every harmful thing that I could to put me out of my misery. I tried marijuana, sex, and pornography, but none of these things could kill me because God had His hands secretively and mightily upon my broken and devalued life. I spent so much time focusing on the word "nothing" that I started to live a disappearing life. When people spoke to me, I lowered my head and shoulders so they would not see me, or rather, they would not see how I saw myself. Oh, yes! I spent all my teen years performing a disappearing act. That is, until Jesus made the true and real me appear. If you find yourself, like me, in this predicament, then you know and understand the pain. Once Satan gets a life to buy into this nothingness theory, that life immediately begins to self-destruct and disappear. Some people commit suicide because they believe that they are nothing and there is no reason to live. Face it! We usually treat ourselves the way we truly feel about ourselves. When a person commits suicide, they are giving you a message as to how they see and feel about themselves. The message they are trying to get across to you is, "I really never existed anyway!" By killing themselves, they are demonstrating that they believed they never had a life in the first place. Thus, in their deaths, one witnesses the mighty and dangerous power of the word "nothing."

I am at a place where I wish I knew then the things that I know now. In fact, if I could travel back in time, I would tell that young, ignorant-of-purpose, empty-headed, and know-it-all boy that God has a way of taking the nothings of this world and giving them shape, form, and fulfillment. If I could go back, I would scream loudly into that frightened boy's ear, "Do not judge yourself by how you look right now! Wait twenty years and take a real, first look into the mirror of who you really are. You are going to love what you see!" Therefore, for those of you in this struggle, I wish to echo these same words to you. Just wait until you see who God has truly meant for you to become. Just you wait!

If you once thought that words cannot hurt anyone, I am sure that you are rethinking that. If allowed in and meditated upon, dangerous words will grow in the soul and fester in the spirit until an entire life is so contaminated that it might never become formed the way God intended. Therefore, be on the listen-out for these words of sabotage-these dangerous words. If you hear them coming, allow your mind to run into the powerful and life-changing words of your awesome God. Never let negative words become your thoughts nor your words. Put them in their place by uttering words from Scripture which dictate God's life to every dead situation opposing yours. A thought formed is an idea conceived; an idea conceived is a belief established; a belief established is an opinion spoken; an opinion spoken is an action created; and an action created is a life formed. You are indeed how you think and what you think. And, what or how you think will let everyone know who you really are.

CHAPTER FOUR

KILLER THOUGHTS

ONE FINE, BEAUTIFUL August day, a young boy named Danny was out in the yard trying to ride his brand new bicycle. While trying the best he could amid the noise of his friends chanting that he could never do it, he fell hard to the pavement and began crying. His father, after hearing a loud sobbing, came running to help his son. When his father realized that his son was all right and saw his son's friends standing around with large crocodile smiles, he asked him if the noisome distractions of his friends had made him fall. With tear-filled eyed, Danny gazed up at his concerned father and said, "Oh, no, Father! It was not my friends' doubting words which made me fall; it was my own loud, doubting thoughts!" You see, Danny fell to the earth not because of outside words but because of hidden, inner thoughts.

My dear friends, sometimes it is not words which sabotage our God-breathed potential but our own misguided and negative thoughts. It is as possible to sin with our words as it is to sin with our thoughts. With your words, you can curse out a difficult boss; but, in your mind, you can do the same. Words are the birth child of thoughts, and thoughts are the hidden womb from which words are conceived, formed, developed, and then launched forth.

The thing that makes thoughts so very dangerous is that they control what comes out of the mouth, what is watched by the eyes, what is listened to through the ears, what is touched by the hands, and what is eaten by the mouth. Therefore, Satan understands that the quickest way to gain control over a person is to control what that person thinks and believes. Please remember that you are only as great or small, positive or negative, confident or insecure as the very thoughts in your mind.

Once thoughts are conceived, they become the basic foundation for all a person's actions. Every crime committed was once a thought conceived. Every sin or evil action was once practiced and performed in the mind of the person who did it. Thus, in the end, thoughts will determine all actions. We are defined through the eyes of others by the actions we take, but we are defined through the lenses of our own eyes by the thoughts we think. Yes, it is definite! Our thoughts define who we are to ourselves.

Since we have proven that thoughts can kill, it should cause us to be very careful about what we think. Thoughts can be birthed from the external words of others, the experiences of one's life, and all the things which one watches. Many times, positive-thinking people can become negative-doing people because they have lived and experienced very negative things. For example, consider a very intelligent and happy sixteen-year-old girl. She is an A-student, does all her homework, and is very responsible. One day, while traveling home from school, she decides to hang out at a friend's house. She enjoys this experience so much that she makes this an after- school ritual. While spending time with this trusted friend, she is introduced to cocaine. After trying it for the first time in her life, she becomes hooked and her grades begin to slip. She becomes so distracted by this addiction that she drops out of school, runs away from home, and is never seen or heard from again. This hypothetical scenario demonstrates how a nega tive environment becomes a negative experience and how that negative experience can have a drastic effect on the thoughts and actions of a positive individual.

Some Christians lose their virginity because they become involved with pornography and begin to think about sex so much that they fall into Satan's mind trap and then into sexual sin. When people are deceived like this, they have long fallen in their own mind. Let's be truthful! Some of the most embar rassing sins we committed were well thought out long before we put them into operation. Therefore, we first fell victim not to the sin but to the sin-producing thought. You had better believe that for every sinful action caught in the open, there is a killer thought hiding in the shadow of a damaged mind.

Many people will never walk with God or have a relation ship with Him, not because of the doubtful words of a friend, but because of the doubting thoughts in their own minds.

There are people who refuse to believe that God is real and that they are sinners in need of His real and saving touch. Thus, in the end, it is their own thoughts that will judge them. These thoughts, if not changed, can result in a person's judgment and death.

So much time in this life and on this earth has been wasted by those who think that they do not belong or have no real purpose for being alive. Because of these thoughts, they never apply themselves to studying, practicing, or even living in a way that moves them beyond where they are or to become more than they are right now. These people have been so depressed in their thinking that they live depressed lives. They will never become great doctors, lawyers, or astronauts, nor will they ever be social and spiritual world-changers. They still live in the same neighborhoods they lived in with their parents from the time they were born. They still hang out on the same street, doing nothing with their lives, because Satan has persuaded their minds into thinking that they are nothing and will never go anywhere except where they are at this moment. In essence, they thought that they were nothing, spent all day thinking about nothing, and thus, they have become nothing. They are being killed by their own thoughts! These people are not killed by stray bullets, but by stray thoughts.

Some people give their lives to vain pursuits because they have killed their minds with vain thoughts. People can be so trapped in lives that accomplish very little or nothing at all because they climb out of the ditch of useless behavior, resulting from useless thoughts. There are some people who are persuaded in their minds that they cannot attain success unless they find others from whose success they can glean. Sometimes they are single mothers who, instead of finding a job or a better education, look for a sugar daddy to pay their way, their rent, and rescue their lives from this misery. Some plan to never work but to depend on government aid for the rest of their lives. These are people who will never feel the awesome rush that comes from fighting to get over negative mountains and becoming positive and well-off role models. Because of their dependent mindsets, they are destined to be failure's doormat. I refuse to believe that those of you who are reading this book could ever settle for such an unfulfilled and defeated life. Dare to live above the reality and results of poverty by thinking above it!

Yes, indeed! As surely as there are dangerous words, there are most definitely killer thoughts! There are moments in the lives of many wherein they are so close to owning that business, changing that poor diet, or consecrating themselves for God's will until the wrong thought shows up. Some thoughts are so crippling that they convince great potential business persons to abort a possible million-dollar business. Many people have died before their time because they never extinguished thoughts about unhealthy eating patterns from their minds and died of heart attacks or diabetes as a result. Then there are some who never walk in the miraculous and life-changing power of God's destiny for them and never bring God's kingdom into their world. They miss out on experiencing God's voice, dominion, and His wonderful Spirit's anointing. These people miss it all!

Saying the wrong things will disrupt every good and godly aspect of a person's life, and thinking terrible thoughts will ensure that these wrong things will be said. If you think it, chances are that it will only be a matter of time until you do it. Always remember that unless a conceived thought is somehow aborted, it will give birth to a child that looks just like it. You must be sure that you hang out with truly positive people. Negative people can only assist you in thinking negatively.

In order for Satan to accomplish his seductive and wicked plans in this earth, he must gather people whose minds are faithless, sinful, perverted, and murderous. Satan knows that in order for murders to increase, he must find people who have spiteful, hateful, and angry thoughts always in their heads. Thus, in order for great evil to exist in this world, Satan and his demonic hosts must find evil minds. This world system consists of Satan using the twisted minds of men and women who have been born in sin in order to create twisted societies. Thus, the wickedness of this present world can only be changed when the mindsets of wicked people change. What a dangerous world! Every sin that is carried out on this planet requires a mind of the same. In order for rape to continue, there must be a rapist mentality. In order for pornographic movies to continue to be made, there must be minds that demand them. Sin still exists because the mindset of sin is still alive. Think about that! The very evil practices which we as believers are designed of God to hate still occur because there are minds that love thinking about them. Wow! The very real and wicked thoughts of people are allowing very evil actions to continue. People are thinking themselves to death!

This world in which we live is not merely a melting pot of many different nations, cultures, and races of people; it is a minefield of invisible thoughts that are trying to find a way into the seen world. Since Adam and Eve abdicated (gave over control) the physical throne of their world to Satan, we find that the majority of the thoughts in the mind realm are evil. Therefore, the physical things we consider dangerous are not what is most dangerous. In other words, people should not just be concerned about guns, but rather with the criminal thoughts of the person holding the gun. By itself, the gun cannot harm anyone. The killer thoughts floating around in the minds of people are the real threat. Therefore, the action of murder is not the only problem; it is also the very thought which produced and caused the murderous act. People are so busy trying to prevent the physically obvious that they are neglecting to tame the hidden and not so obvious. If people would become more concerned with what and how they think, then this world would be a safe and more productive place. Dangerous and unhealthy thoughts are killing people in massive numbers.

It is true that it is far easier to catch criminals than it is to capture mental thoughts. This is why wrong thoughts are so dangerous. For every ten murderers caught, one thousand thoughts of murder are born. Because of this, there is no way for any physical or human police force to stop the crime of dangerous thoughts. These killer thoughts, used by Satan, continue to multiply at such a rapid pace that the sinful world of mankind has become fatigued just thinking about the actions caused or that shall be caused by them. Think about it! How do you defeat something that can't be seen by human eyes, captured by human hands, stopped by guns, or incarcerated by the police? You surely cannot accomplish this with human strength or ingenuity; instead, it is only by the power and presence of the Holy Ghost that these things can be defeated.

Since the time of mankind's first sin and right up to our present generation, the vile thoughts of mankind have been an ever-increasing source of humanity's failure, misfortune, and destruction. Even though this has been the case, people all over the world blame God for their terrible lot in life. If a plane crashed tomorrow, they ask why God allowed it. If someone in their family gets shot, they ask how a good God could allow such a terrible evil. Sometimes planes crash because engineers fixing those planes mistakenly leave a damaged part on the plane or a manufacturer develops an inferior product. Sometimes people get shot because of criminals not just carrying a gun but also a criminal way of thinking. Please be assured that God does not do these evil works! Instead, evil deeds always start with the wicked thinking or perverted thought lives of messed-up, spiritually broken human beings.

Our very own destructive thoughts are silently killing God's vision and our own personal dreams for our lives. As you continue to live on this earth, you will notice that people are only as big, successful, effective, committed to God, and strong as they are able to think. Therefore, failure or success is simply a matter of how people think, which determines how they see themselves. When we fail, it is because we have already failed within our own minds. On the other hand, if we succeed, it is because we have already committed to that success in our minds. When people give up on life, you had better believe that they have already settled it in their minds and have concluded that there is no hope or reason to continue fighting. Great boxers and great athletes know that the challenger is not just their outside opponent but also their inner thoughts. Many races have been lost because an athlete had already visualized losing that particular race in his or her own head. Many boxers have gotten knocked out in a fight because they were already knocked out even before the fight began by the thoughts in their heads.

Most things can only happen for us if we are brave enough to believe with our own minds that they could. Therefore, if you want to break people's destinies, you have to break it in the arena of their thought life. Satan, to this very day, has been defeating entire generations of God's people at the thought level. He is able to so manipulate all that they see, hear, taste, and experlience that they have based their entire lives not on faith but solely on their senses. Some have gone to a doctor and were told that they have some blood-born or genetic illness, and they immediately accept this word and develop a sick mind right up to their own death. It is amazing how many Christians are not even standing in faith and spiritually fighting anymore. Many of us have accepted the wrong end, simply because we allowed our minds to believe in a false beginning. So many Christians have entered the wrong marriage because the people whom they had thought they were marrying, turned out to be the very opposite of who they really were. Many of the sisters have been hoodwinked into marrying some very abusive, lazy, and trifling men. On the flip side of the coin, many brothers have gotten caught in the same visual and mental trap. My friends, just because something appears good on the surface does not mean that it is truly good enough to allow into the depth of your soul. We must no longer allow our own messed-up thoughts to dictate the outcome of our destiny. One of the most dangerous things we can do is to hire, marry, or fellowship with anyone just because we happen to think that they are honest or that they are the right one. We must ensure that we get the God-revealed facts! We must be sure to check with God before we evaluate anyone with our own minds. The only way we can be tricked into a bad purchase or life investment is if we first agree on it with our mind.

I wish to tell you that I am a living witness and a testimony to the real danger hidden within these killer thoughts. In my opinion, bad thoughts are as dangerous as trigger-happy gun owners. They are as threatening as terrorists carrying nuclear explosives. Some years ago, before I got married, I was seeking God and readying myself for that blessed event which I would share with the love of my life-my first, present, and only wife. Everything was going well! I had embraced God's Spirit-led life, and she and I were keeping ourselves away from all sexual experience. We were striving to present ourselves to each other, untouched and holy. While I was so busy focusing on our future life together, I neglected to cast out of my mind the intense desire to kiss her for the first time. Now you might be thinking silently to yourself, "How bad could one kiss be?"

Well I have to admit, I felt the same way as you. I let that little seed thought linger in my mind because I did not see the dangers hidden within it. Sometimes we never see the train coming because we are blinded by its light. Instead of realizing that this little thought was going to lead me to greater destructive actions, I just allowed the thought to lead me. In hindsight, I wish that I had committed this thought to the Lord and allowed His all-seeing and all-knowing Spirit to test it and reveal to me its truest motive. However, all my sight was tied up in the thought of that first kiss. So, just how dangerous might a simple one-time kiss be? Well, I will tell you! That one kiss that I gave to my soon-to-be wife led me down a sensual path of moving from a kiss, to a deeper kiss; from a deeper kiss, to an unholy touch; and from an unholy touch, to an almost sexual experience. I felt so dirty after falling to this kind of behavior that I repented before God and took time away from my then-fiancee until it was time for our wedding. Because I was so careless, I had tarnished much of the beauty which God had planned for my life and hers. However, thanks be to God that He is able to recreate beauty out of the mental and physical garbage piles we allow into our lives. So, you can definitely see how one wrong thought can lead to many wrong actions. Believe me when I tell you that it only takes one killer thought to ruin an awesome, God-appointed life. thoughts in your mind. Thoughts are like the wind; unless a barrier is put in place to block them, they will blow wherever they please and will be hard to control. In order to transform pessimists, one must change their thinking. In order to transform sin-sick people, one must replace every detestable and sick thought within their mind with thoughts of a greater good. Only by the birth, nurturing, and transforming power of the Holy Ghost can this kind of radical and mind-altering change occur. No psychologist nor psychiatrist can go deep into the sinful, psychotic regions of the human soul and trans-form its messed-up nature into something new that has never existed before. Only the Word of God and the Spirit of God can venture to such a deep place and deliver such a twisted and tormented mindset! It is only through the blood of Jesus Christ. Your old way of thinking, once you would have entered the kingdom of God by grace and faith, must be transformed. In other words, the thoughts of your before-Christ mindset had failed your life so badly that you were in need of a drastic and spiritual overhaul. Jesus not only introduced you to the Holy Ghost, His agent of change, but Jesus is now working in you to erase the mindset devised by Satan in order to kill you. In the same way that you would not believe that a murderer holding a gun in his hand would not harm you, do not ever believe that your old negative way of thinking could ever do anything to save, repair, protect, or bring you into God's complete and finished design for you. It most certainly cannot and will not!

Whether we want to believe it or not, killer thoughts are lurking behind the doorway of our minds and must be banished from the living rooms of our God-made spiritual houses. In order to evict old sinful, poisonous killer thoughts, we must create new and righteous ones. In order to create new and righteous thoughts, one must put into the mind new and righteous words. Furthermore, in order to put new and righteous words into the mind, we must surely study and meditate on the very potent, healing, life-changing, mind-altering, demon-chasing, and Satan-expelling Word of God. If you want to overcome any and all ugly and sinful activities, you must concentrate on developing intimacy with the Holy Ghost through the Bible, prayer, praise, worship, and fasting. Also, if you want to be a better spouse and not just a bitter one, then allow the sweet aroma of the nature or fruit of the Spirit of God to be your everyday course of action and practice. Exchange your broken and ruined imperfect thoughts for God's beautiful and glorious thoughts. Allow God's powerful nature so deep within your new and living Spirit man, that Satan could not remove it himself. Therefore, think like God! Act in accordance to His will! But never think and be the same old sinful you again!

CHAPTER FIVE

THE MIND OF THE DEFEATED

DEFEAT IS ALWAYS 100 percent mental before it is 100 percent physical! You cannot win at anything if, before you have even attempted, you are convinced that you will lose! Defeat comes to those who refuse to accept any other possibility!

There were days in my life and in my God walk that I just did not believe I could handle an assignment from God or that the plans of God for my life would ever be fulfilled in my lifetime. It was at this very low time in my life that I realized that merely sitting back and accepting defeat was not helping me at all. On my first-ever college quiz, I got an F, and I began to doubt even the purpose of God in sending me to college. You see, I was still operating in the mindset of an F-student-the student that I was in high school and who barely made it to graduation. Oh, yes! I began to fail at the college level because my loser and already defeated mindset was very much alive in me and still in control. This mindset did not care that I was sent to this particular college by God to prepare for the work of the ministry; nor was it concerned with how anointed

I was. The mindset of defeat's goal was to live, thrive, and totally crush all God-breathed potential in me.

Now, I have to warn you that this type of mindset is not developed overnight and neither will it simply fade away overnight, just because you might be walking with your God. Oh, no! This mindset must be overpowered and challenged to change by God's Holy Spirit and His powerful and instructional words. In addition, you must constantly allow God's nature within your living spirit to quietly and forcefully kill the presence of that defeated mindset.

There are some things you should know concerning how a defeated mind is made and sustained, how it looks, and the damage it will inevitably cause. First, a mind of defeat is not born, it must be made! A defeated mind is first shaped by what I call generational flaws. Every generation before you in your family tree carried with it, and inevitably passed onto the generation after it, many immoral and sin flaws. Each sin flaw practiced by your great-grandmother or great-grandfather has been passed down to your parents and will one day attempt to become the object of your defeat. Therefore, whatever sin defeat has been experienced by your parents will soon become your struggle and your fight. Some people struggle with cigarette and nicotine addiction because that addiction was introduced a generation before them. Maybe the grandfather was a heavy tobacco smoker. Then, that addiction became so strong in the bloodline that just about all the men and women after grandpa developed that same taste for smoking and became addicts themselves. Whether you choose to believe it or not, the addictions of one generation will usually become the weaknesses of another. The first generation's flaws can so weaken the generation after it that this second generation will develop within itself a very defeated mindset. There are some women who have fallen into the trap of having sex out of wedlock because they might have followed the example set by their parents before them. These women have already defeated their own potential, locking themselves away behind the bars of their parent's failures. So, before they even fight to keep that precious gift of God, their virginity, they have already lost it in their own defeated minds and may, quite possibly, end up pregnant like others before them.

In another case, let us visualize a man who has a father in jail for murder. The father has always been known to have a very bad temper. Now that he is in prison, his son begins to lash out in anger at the world. Therefore, he simply gives his mind over to every angry impulse. This young man has already mapped out his entire future by gazing too long into the messed-up present situation of his father. His father's failure has now become the weakness and defeat of the son's mind, and it will only be a matter of time before the son becomes the spitting image of his father's failure. All of us will battle these generational flaws. Whether we are saved or a sinner, we must face the reality that we are constantly defining and redefining ourselves based upon the records of those who have gone before us.

Some of us assume that because we look just like our parents, we are doomed to live the very lives of our parents. Thus, the defeat which we now carry came from the vision of the defeated lives of parents or grandparents who came before us. Some people have become sexual molesters, because they were sexually molested by a father or mother or other relative. The act was so emotionally wounding that the victim, years later, developed the same thought patterns and harmed another child. This new child molester became a monster because he or she allowed the parent's monster to become his or her nightmare. Now this individual is locked behind prison bars, not just because of the act of sexual molestation but because their defeated mind could not shake the vile thoughts of a future act of molestation. Countless lives have been ruined because many were convinced that the apple cannot ever fall far from the tree. Satan is banking on this information to work; he will have to work less to destroy humankind if they are destroying themselves. I am a living witness that through Jesus Christ, not only does the apple not have to be like the tree from which it fell, but it can actually become an orange. Jesus can help us change our nature in such a radical way that the generational flaws found in the very blood of our forefathers need never be found in our minds.

The second factor that makes a defeated mind is the use of depressive words. Many of you, from the very instant that you were born and then able to understand words have encountered a satanic plan designed to suppress all of God's potential in you and eliminate every thought of self-worth. Satan's plan, as you grew up, was to cause depressive words to be spoken either directly to you or around you. What an aggressive plan! Satan knows that words carry the power of persuasion and influence. He knows that these two powers within words will either cause a life to become great or small, wise or foolish, and filled with faith or empty with doubt. Words are powerful! While growing up, some of you might have been told that you were stupid. At the first hearing of this word, maybe you were not even moved. However, after years of hearing it, your grades started to slip. Then, all of a sudden, you no longer thought that you were beautiful or attractive. So, you began to not care how you looked, and you became a mess when you dressed yourself for school. You hated to look in the mirror because you saw yourself as someone of no value or worth. If this was or even is your life's experience now, I want you to know that God does not make junk! He might make great beauty out of junk, but He makes no junk at all. You have just been lied to by a depressive word sent directly from the mouth of Satan himself. For others of you, the depressive words did not come from outside of you but were always within your mind. Some of you have been listening to the repeat recording of the song, "You're No Good." You believe that everyone else can get good grades, but that you're just not good enough. You think that everyone else is good enough to attend college, but you should not even try because you are just no good. Maybe you believe that everyone else will find Mister or Miss Right, but you never will because you are no good. What a great lie you have come to believe about yourself! There are so many people, and even Christians, who will never amount to anything, not because they were not designed to by God but because they listened too long to the wrong depressive words. Please get it into your head that whatever you listen to will eventually shape what you become. A defeated mind surely starts at the mouth of depressive words. I believe that we have all heard in our lifetime some word designed to depress even our relationship with God. In fact, the words, "Why would God?" can be some very depressing words. There are some people who have an ugly frame of mind and imply or directly ask, "Why would God use you?" I believe that many of you do not ever share Jesus Christ with your family because you are afraid that some will wonder why God would use you. On the other hand, there are some of you whose past life was so immoral and sinful that you are asking yourself why God would even call you. This type of question has held many people back from following Jesus Christ, developing great life-changing medicine, writing God-inspired, life-changing books, or just making a difference in the lives of others. If you do not believe that God has any business using you, then you do not believe that you have any business living. And, if you believe that you have no business living, then your life's worth and all of God's possibilities for your life will never be made alive. You would have ceased to exist! Any life on this planet that believes it is of no value to God or to others is really not even alive. Sadly enough, it has not yet lived! In the end, a depressed life filled with depressive words is no life worth living at all. Jesus Christ, by his Holy Spirit, dares you never to live like this!

The third and final cause of a defeated mind is that of defeated companions. Yes, readers! A person's choice of friends is directly related to the type of mindset that this person will have. If you hang around fools-people who have no vision of God nor where they are going-in time, you will also begin to lose sight of all that your life can be for God and for humankind. Friends with defeated minds have no sense of their own true worth and will surely never assist you in finding yours. These are people in your life who live only for the day. They work to party and play and some of them do not work at all. Defeated companions never finish anything that they start, nor are they willing to start anything worth finishing. One day, their mindset will become your very life's mission statement. Please realize that these people's lives do not serve as examples of great and significant ministry, work, or invention. If their lives cannot inspire you to be more, do more, and seek God more, then you will have an empty, uninspired mind and life. Every human being on this planet is designed to be inspired. The mind and spirit that are Holy Spirit-inspired will move the earth itself. It is when we are uninspired by God and by His chosen people that we cease to be alive and fulfilled.

People can only inspire you if they themselves have been inspired. Therefore, friends with defeated minds have no inspiration and can only pass onto you a mind of the same. Think about this! Can someone who has never finished high school be an excellent inspiration for you to finish? Now, they can try, but the answer is a resounding, "No!" You might listen if they were to lecture you about the importance of getting a good education, but the noise of their failure and subsequent school dropout would drown out the sensible words they would be speaking. We tend to respect people who live what they speak more than those who do not. Would you listen to a person who has no bank account, savings plan, investment portfolio, or job tell you how to become a millionaire? You would probably say, "No way!" So then, why do we keep friends in our lives who only live defeated and do not really care to learn how to win? If you are believing God to heal you of cancer, you do not need someone around telling you that it is impossible. If you are trying to kick a drug addiction, you definitely do not need a person beside you injecting a needle filled with liquefied cocaine into his or her arm. Once you decide to live above the dust of this world's wickedness, you are going to have to let go of friends who are comfortable playing in dirt. You will never become an eagle if you allow people with the mindsets of turkeys access to your life.

Now that you know how the defeated mind is made, let us sneak a peak at how the defeated mind looks. The first quality of a defeated mind which reveals that defeat has already occurred is a lack of faith. Show me a mind lying dormant with the stench of defeat all over it, and I will show you a person who has never had faith or whose faith has become silenced due to worldly pressures. According to the biblical story of Jesus on the tempestuous sea with his disciples, a storm arose and threatened the safety of the disciples. After Jesus rebuked the sea and the wind, he then rebuked them for their lack of faith. Because they lacked this awesome, God-inspired commodity, they had already seen their deaths by way of this storm. Frozen with terror, their minds no longer believed that they would make it to the other side of the lake, so they had begun to accept that their end was near. But this was never what Jesus had planned for them. Isn't it amazing how we as Christians sometimes allow our own minds to believe a false reality which God has never made for us? We are so faithless at times in our walk with God that we are quick to admit that a sickness must be God's will for us or, perhaps, we will never get over the mountain of poverty because that is just what God has designed for our lives. Where there is no faith, no satanic mountains can be moved. A person having no faith connection with God through the rebirth of a living spirit will eventually live a defeated life, even in the midst of physical human successes. It is quite possible to attain millions and still be spiritually poor and thus be emotionally defeated and bankrupt. This is why there are so many suicidal, depressed, and frustrated millionaires in this world. You must understand that neither physical wealth nor fame are complete and whole objects. Sometimes, in fact, the more known that you are, the more lonely you will become. People who have no other help but that of humankind in this earth will fail even as those physical arms of human strength fail. Therefore, faith is vital for victory in all aspects of life because it is the only thing powerful enough to connect a person to the Almighty God. And when earth fails, this God is well able to step his eternity-sized feet into your life situation and change its outcome from defeat into victory, from sadness into great joy, from rejection into acceptance, and from doubt into great hope. However, people whose minds have already thrown in the towel, perhaps due to the loss of a job, a close relative, a promotion, or a house, will never taste the wonderful fruits of God's victory tree because they refuse to plant the seeds of faith in order to reap the tree of faith. If faith is absent, even the greatest or wealthiest life is assured defeat. In fact, defeat has already sprung to life!

Another reason a person without God-released faith is a defeat-minded person is because without faith one cannot see far; one can only see things up close as they appear and not what they can become in the future. A person without faith can never please God and, therefore, will never have access to the only power that can move all mountains and obstacles of defeat. Furthermore, without faith there is no vision, and without a vision life becomes such a risk that one misstep or wrong turn can bring an end to that life. You had better realize that the safest way to overcome defeat is to fill your mind with God, His faith-filled words, and His faith-manifesting Holy Spirit. Faith is the check, rich enough to pay in full the debt of defeat. Won't you cash in on it today?

By now you probably realize that any mind without faith is already defeated. However, this is not the only missing quality associated with the look of a defeated mind. A lack of self-control is very apparent in the mind of a defeated person. Self-control is the ability for an individual to exercise any level of restraint in any given situation. Therefore, people who are able to control their thoughts will be able to control their actions; and people who can skillfully and successfully control their own actions will be better able to shape their own future. For example, if Sally is able to control her appetite for fatty foods, then she could probably avoid clogged arteries which could end up leading to a heart attack. Many illnesses, which people develop within their bodies, really began with a mind lacking control and concern about what their bodies ate, drank, smoked, or practiced. Thus, the lack of self-control would have aided in the subsequent physical breakdown of those person's own bodies. It is truly a scary thing when your out-of-control mind is your worst enemy. Please be sure to also note that everything we eat with our mouths and digest with our stomachs, we have already eaten with our minds. Therefore, if we truly become what we eat, then this is because we eat what we think. The defeated mind is one in which self is never in control. This is a mind that says, "Self, although AIDS is out there and you never truly know who has it, still go ahead and have sex with this perfectly good-looking stranger. Go ahead, take the chance. She doesn't look like a person who could be HIV positive!" Well, here is a dumb thought! But you know, people think like this everyday. This person is going to one day wake up, find himself in a doctor's office, and blame God for allowing him to have contracted AIDS or HIV. Listen very carefully! A mind without self-control, or God's control, is probably one of the most dangerous and explosive elements known to humankind. A lack of self-control is the equivalent of a trigger-happy cop with a loaded gun in the middle of the night. You should realize that anything moving too suddenly is going to get shot. We have a very serious problem in both the church and the world of sinners when we live among people who will do anything and everything that they want to do, without any restraint. There are some people who, having already contracted a sexually transmitted disease, will intentionally have sex with unsuspecting victims to get revenge on having caught this disease themselves. What a disgusting mess! You see, they have given themselves over to a nature that is without love for humanity and has no self-control to protect others from their own destruction. A person without self-control is not under the same limitations as you or me. Just because you might be walking with God and living a life that is pure and God-controlled does not mean that everyone around you is doing the same. The defeated mind, having no self-control, will participate in a great deal of harm. Many murders have occurred simply because someone lost control over his or her emotions and started stabbing or shooting another individual. Thus, the seed of sabotage easily grew into a tree of murder because of a mind lacking the correct controls. Let me attempt, by the Holy Ghost, to paint you a very graphic picture of how one mind, devoid of self-control, can influence another to think and act in the same manner. Here we have Jim. He is a playboy and international) ladies' man. One day Jim meets Janet, a married woman who is going through a rough patch in her marriage. Jim, having no respect for the sanctity of marriage and no self-control in his entire being, convinces Janet to allow him to escort her back to her home. While at her home, Jim begins to seduce Janet and, due to her vulnerable state of mind, she loses all self-restraint and has sex with Jim right in the bed upon which she and her husband sleep. After the sinful deed is done, Janet begins to sob uncontrollably, realizing what she has truly done. Suddenly, before she sheds one last tear, her husband Dan enters the bedroom. Upon seeing his wife and her lover together on the bed, he goes into a fit of rage. He quickly gets his gun that he keeps in the nightstand and opens fire on Jim and Janet. Blood is everywhere, as both Jim and Janet lay dead. When Dan finally comes to his right mind and realizes the terrible thing he has done, he turns the gun on himself and ends his life. This story represents a very graphic display of how Jim's lack of self-control led to Janet's failure as a faithful wife and inevitably, to Dan's out-of-control rage, the murders of Jim and Janet, and his own suicidal death. Surely, we must understand that our lapse in self-control can cause someone else to lose control. Therefore, one defeated mind without self-control may cause serious damage to anyone who will listen or be influenced by it.

Any great athlete will tell you that before you can win in any sport, you must condition your mind first and then you can condition your body. Thus, your mind is really the source from which your body will draw either the correct information or the wrong information. In other words, if athletes' minds are conditioned to give their bodies the correct information concerning the right foods to eat, then they have a better chance of winning because they would have more fit and healthier bodies. Now, a good way to get athletes to fail at any sport would be to prevent them from exercising self-control in what they eat.

Christians who do not exercise the God-implanted nature of self-control will never truly grow to maturity in God. God makes more of Himself known and gives more of Himself only to those who lose all of themselves. When believers cast down their out-of-control egos and put to death their lack-of-self-control actions, then the Holy Spirit will take them to places of spiritual ecstasy with their God. You cannot truly walk with God and experience supernatural miracles in your life if you cannot bring your mind and body under God's control. The mind that has no self-control will never truly allow God to be in control and will never experience an overwhelming victory over the sins and faults of the past. The only way to break free from the mistakes of the generations before you is to allow God to develop a different mindset in you. Since the majority of sinful activities within our families probably occurred because of a lack of self-control, in order to break this vicious sin-curse cycle we must allow God's nature to control that which the previous generations would not. Remember, your greatest spiritual victory is just one God-given, self-controlled action away!

Show me a mind without self-control or God's nature in control, and I will show you a person who cannot be ruled by the laws of man or the laws of God's kingdom. People who cannot bring rule to themselves will never be ruled by anyone or anything else. Nations are in trouble today and great sophisticated societies are in disarray because of a handful of people who never allowed God to bring control into their lives. In other words, those that will not be controlled, cannot be controlled! Therefore, the world will continue to have criminals and addicts because there will always exist, within the borders of these nations, people with mindsets lacking self-control. In today's world, there are many alcoholics, drug addicts, and sex addicts being made everyday. There are those who believe that a person who is addicted to any legal or illegal substance has become so after continuous use of these substances. However, the Holy Spirit has revealed to me that an addict is not made by years of substance abuse but is instead made in the first taste, smoke, or snort of that addictive substance. It only takes the first taste, and then the hunger is born and the addiction is sealed. Now, this first taste actually does not happen within the mouth, but within the mind. The mind first desires to taste that drug or that nicotine, and then the mouth simply complies with the mind's desire. Therefore, the failure of an addicted life first begins in the defeated mind devoid of self-control. If you want to overcome the addictions of your family, you must allow God to enter your life and help you develop a mind that does not even want the first taste of that alcoholic or drug-laced substance. Once you bring your mindset for the first taste under God's taste control, then you will be able to destroy every addictive taste that would have marked your future destiny. Furthermore, if you want to beat a negative addictive habit, never start it at all. And, if you wish to never start an addictive habit, control your mind with a God-breathed habit!

The next unfortunate look of the defeated mind is that of worry. A defeated mind is what the Holy Spirit terms a worrier and not a warrior. Worry is one of the most dangerous and hidden enemies of any soul and of the great God-breathed potential locked away in the new and living spirit of the believer. When people worry, it signifies that before they have even attempted to fight, they have already admitted defeat in their mind. For example, consider Susan. Susan is about to take her SATs; all school year long, she has been making As. However, despite her academic achievements, she fears that the SAT examination might be too difficult for her. Therefore, instead of studying with confidence days before the impending exam, she spends that time cringing with worry. She worries so much that she loses sleep as well as most of the information that she had studied. Soon, the fateful day of the SAT arrives, and Susan manages to finish all of her questions. Sometime later, Susan receives the results of her exam. As she glances at the paper, she falls to the ground in tears. She discovers that she has failed miserably. What has happened to Susan can happen to anyone. You see, Susan spent so much time worrying that she failed the SAT mentally before she had even taken it physically. This is the dangerous sabotage which worry causes. Worry is a written check to a bank account that is overdrawn and void of money. The instant you cash this check, it will leave you with a bounce experience and no ability to possess any of earth's goods or heaven's wealth. In fact, even our Lord Jesus Christ discouraged the act of worry. God knows that if the human mind is submerged in the flood tides of worry, then it will not be able to swim above the riptides of sinful, satanic distractions. Worry is like tying an anchor to a swimmer's ankle. In no time, even the strongest or fastest swimmer will be pulled under the water because of the heaviness of that anchor. Therefore, worry is my anchor, and it is your anchor. Worry will never lead you to that promotion for which you have been waiting during your ten years at your job. You would be so crippled by the blows of worry that your effec tiveness on the job would actually begin to suffer. You might forget to do work that has been assigned to you, and this would cause your managers to lose confidence in you. Worry will always position you on the bottom rung of the ladder, looking up as others climb to the top of manage ment and sit on the thrones of pay increases. Face it, you will never win playing for the team of worry. The mind that worries has already sabotaged its own potential and has blocked the power of God's Spirit from working within and flowing through its life.

When the mind is overtaken by intense worrying, it begins to view life in a very twisted way. Worry causes us to look at shadows and give them form and power over us. An example of this is found in the New Testament in the story of Jesus Christ bringing calm to the storm. According to this biblical fact, Jesus had told his disciples to get into a boat and travel across the sea to the other side. While they were on this vessel, Jesus fell asleep and a terrible storm came up, beating hard against their little boat. The disciples panicked in horror! Fearing for their lives, they awoke Jesus from his much-needed rest. When He awoke, He rebuked the wind and the waves and then His very own disciples for having no faith at the time in which faith was definitely required. This awesome story reveals to us many truths concerning life and God's kingdom. However, we will concentrate on one main revelation from the bowels of this story. The disciples were so frozen with worry, they viewed the storm outside the boat as much larger than Jesus Christ who was right in their boat. Their vision was so twisted that they did not even remember that Jesus had told them that they would be going over to the other side. They should have remembered that this was the same Jesus who healed the sick by one word. This was the same Jesus who performed miracles that no man in their day could have done. However, they had forgotten Jesus Christ's miraculous track record because they accepted the record of a storm instead. In essence, when we worry, we are doing exactly what these New Testament disciples had done. Worry rnakes us believe that the storms of debt, sickness, divorce, hurt, death, and rejection are too big for an awesome God to handle. Every time we worry, we are indirectly telling God that we do not truly believe that He will come to our aid or that He is able to help in the time of trouble. Worry views God as the grasshopper and our problems as the giant. This is not good! Worry is an insult thrown directly into the face of our great God. So, stop worrying! Worry is not your friend. It is, most definitely, not your God. Therefore, be a warrior and not a worrier!

Another look worn by a person with the mind of defeat is that of extreme bitterness. Show me a person with a bitter attitude, and I will reveal to you a person who has given up on God, dreams, goals, or life itself. Sometimes when people lose sporting events, they might become overwhelmed with bitterness. I am sure that none of us likes to lose! No one likes the feeling of losing anything. Bitterness is usually a direct birth child of the womb of loss. In this world today, there are so many defeated people. They have been so beaten up by bills, sickness, loss of jobs, failed dreams, spousal rejection, and a host of wounds that have left them out of breath and in the pits of the agony of defeat. No wonder the world is such a cold and bitter place! The number of defeated minds, or minds that think they are defeated, determines how much bitterness there will be in a nation or society. People who are bitter will never encourage or inspire others to great heights of godliness, creativity, or success. Someone who is filled with the sickness of bitterness will not be able to bring healing to someone who has been broken by the harshness of a bitter life. In the church today, there are bitter preachers, worship pastors, and intercessory leaders who are not helping to bring healing and wholeness to the believers of Christ. Instead, they are inflicting more wounds on the Lord's people and turning them away from the church and even from the Christian faith. This brutality must stop! Bitterness cannot heal. It must be healed first. A bitter life is a defeated life, and it will bring others down into the pit of discouragement along with it. Bitterness sets like cement Within the mind and seals in resentment, discouragement, and hatred. This dangerous three-pronged state of thinking vvill unleash upon the church, or the world, people who will do nothing to encourage faith, increase love, or inspire true change. All that will occur is the reality of defeat! In life, a losing mentality can never birth and raise a winning mentality. Do not allow bitter-minded people to speak their poisonous words of doubt, prejudice, hate, or lies into your mind. They will only seek to sabotage the awesome potential of God in your life. There are so many Christians whose faith has been hijacked by the spiritual terrorists of harmful words spoken through the mouths of defeated and bitter people.

Another look of the defeated mind is the face of jealousy. Jealousy is that intense, passionate hate of someone's victory or success. This is a seed of sabotage found in the dark, hidden caves of the defeated mind. Since defeated mind's reality is that it cannot succeed at anything, then it will hate all those who believe that they can or have already attained success. One reason for the many jealous people in the world, and even in the church, is their belief that since they have failed (whether they tried or not), everyone else should either not try or not succeed if they do try. Have you ever stopped to consider that maybe the reason some people on your job, in your school, or even in your family do not like to be around you is because they do not like your success? Maybe they feel threatened by your passion for being the best that you can be in everything assigned to you. In this life, there are some who hate winners only because they see themselves as losers. Therefore, since many of them have long given up on winning at anything, they are praying that others fail at everything. Whether you believe it or not, this type of thinking exists.

Jealousy is a deadly two-headed snake that will not only hate others for their success but will attempt to cause their failure. The first deadly part of jealousy will produce so much hate in the defeated mind that this person will never encourage another person nor celebrate another's victory. In the Bible, a man named Cain, whose sacrifice was not accepted by God, hated his brother Abel because his was accepted. Cain was so filled with jealousy that he despised his own brother's success. In fact, Cain killed Abel in an attempt to kill Abel's success. This is the second head of the two-headed serpent known as jealousy. Some people, like Cain, are so intensely spiteful of the blessing of others that they will try to wreck that person's life. They may spread lies and rumors, attempt to get them fired, or even murder them because of jealousy. Therefore, people who live defeated lives are very dangerous to those who live victorious lives because they may do anything within their power to bring down successful people. Instead of trying to get a job to support themselves, some people would rather steal from those who are making money by hard work. In other words, if I am too lazy and defeated to make my own wealth, I will just hate all those who are striving to make a good financial life for themselves. Thus, it would be easier for me to steal their success than to work for my own. This is the way the defeated and jealous mind thinks. The jealous mind thinks that because it did not get into college (even though it did not apply itself in school), then no one else should be able to get into college. I am persuaded that one of the reasons we are so quick to talk badly about other people is due to the fact that, somewhere deep inside of us, we do not believe that we could have done what they have accomplished. Sometimes, when we see ourselves as failures, it is hard for us to want to celebrate or recognize the legitimate successes of others. This is where jealousy enters, and if we are not careful, jealousy can so consume all our time and energy that we will find no time to become winners ourselves. Therefore, by hating another person's success, I am actually killing my own!

Well, since you realize how the defeated mind looks, we will take a closer look at how the defeated mind is sustained. If you want to destroy anything that is destructive, you have to discover what is sustaining it. In order to kill a tree, you have to destroy the root system of that tree. It is the roots that sustain the life of any tree. In the same breath, if you wish to defeat the mind of defeat, you must have a clear revelation of what causes it to live. Please know that every thing, whether it be human, animal, or even thoughts, is alive. Therefore, a defeated mind carries defeated thoughts within, and these thoughts are alive. Anything that is alive must be fed to continue living. We will now take a careful look at things that keep a defeated mind alive.

The first element keeping a defeated mind on life support is ignorance. The word ignorance means a lack of knowledge or correct knowledge. Ignorance continues to feed a defeated mind by preventing any knowledge of victory from entering. Think about it. Many people continue to have defeated minds because they have no knowledge that they can do any better. Thus, ignorance causes people to believe that they have no options. Some people do not know that they have a winning potential within them and a God-given talent or skill that would make them very successful in this life. Therefore, they never tap into that potential and never accomplish something great or life-changing. Thus, what they do not know is what defeats them.

Many individuals decide to drop out of school because they are ignorant to the truth that some students are late intellectual bloomers. Therefore, because they are making Fs right now, they assume that they will always be F-students and decide to quit in defeat. These students judged their future greatness as being small because of their present failures. Oh, yes! It is so easy for us to condemn our future destiny because of the present ignorance of our minds. This kind of ignorance allows a mind of defeat to live a very long time and cause a great amount of damage. It is very sad to have greatness from God within but never know it because you have been blinded by the fog of ignorance. We miss the wonderful beauty of a God-appointed victorious life within us because we simply do not see the supernatural life of God that is inside our inner spirit. We can only see ourselves based upon what we know about ourselves. If we do not realize that we have the potential to live victoriously, then we will never believe that we are, nor will we ever be victorious. Therefore, this lack of knowledge leads us to live defeated lives,

The second life support to the mind of defeat is a lack of spiritual (God-inspired) vision. What we are unable to see, whether by natural sight or by supernatural faith, we will never possess or become. Defeated people lack God's insight into what they can truly become and, more important, into how God truly sees them. The world and your own failures seek to give you a false sense of your true abilities. With God's vision, however, you would know that you are designed to be much greater than what physical eyes can see. You should realize that whatever we see becomes what we will eventually believe, and what we believe deter-mines the *way* that we will live. Defeated people have not yet put on the eyeglasses of God. They still wear the damaged lenses of human frailty and satanic deception. Therefore, their own broken vision of themselves is killing every God-purposed potential locked up within them. If we do not allow the Holy Spirit to give us heaven's vision, we will truly see ourselves as nothing more than passing shadows. We would never see ourselves as having substance and form. Our defeat is only as real as our vision. If you could visualize yourself, just for one minute, as being a predator and not a prey, a success and not a failure, and a lion and not a weak lamb, then you could no longer live defeated. Defeat only comes to those who can see nothing but defeat. In the Old Testament, when the children of Israel were about to cross over the Jordan River, they failed to enter the land because some of the spies saw themselves as grasshoppers and saw their enemies as giants. Because of this, an entire generation of God's people died in the wilderness. You see, they lived based upon how they saw themselves. Because of their lack of God-inspired vision, God's destined promise was lost to thousands. It is impossible to possess God's goods without having God's vision! Now, one can clearly see how a lack of spiritual vision will always feed the dangerous defeated mind.

Another sustainer of a defeated mind is a person's negative environment. Yes, indeed! Where a person was born and where a person lives greatly influence how a person thinks or acts. According to Psalm 51, God's servant David was repenting for a sin he had committed and wrote about being born in sin and made in iniquity. David was attempting to portray that it was so easy for him to sin because sin's ability was born into him and that his very environment helped breed and support sin. This Bible reference stands as proof that sometimes people have defeated minds because that is all that they have experienced in their world. Many people are poor in this world because they developed the mindset from growing up poor that they could never be rich. Many have become thieves because they have been conditioned by years of living in a neighborhood filled with criminals. Millions of teenagers are seeking to have sex or have already had sex simply because all they see and hear around them is sex and sensuality. It has become so bad that, for some girls and boys, virginity is considered something embarrassing and shameful. Can you believe this?

People's minds, whether they know it or not, are constantly being conditioned by their environment. Some of us never achieve great things because we hang around very small thinkers. The people we hang out with will influence the way we think. If we keep friends who are racially prejudice, we are going to begin to think the same *way*. If a single person, who is trying to remain a virgin until marriage, hangs out with sexually active people, that person will soon be persuaded to have sex. There is no doubt in my mind! Our thoughts are shaped by the people we hang around and the places we go. A defeated mind will always be kept alive as long as there are oppressed, drug-filled, poor, hate-filled, and depressed communities. And since there will always be communities like this, there will always be people who have no hope, integrity, passion, and initiative. People die every day having never realized their full potential. They have been fooled in their minds by the messed-up situation in which they lived. What a sad state of affairs! This is why Jesus gives us a new birth. He is replacing the image of where we were first born by infusing us with an entirely different life and locale. Therefore, instead of being born in a negative and broken community on earth, we have now been given a zip code that is heaven itself. Jesus knows that a defeated environment will give birth to a defeated mind unless a victorious and free environment replaces it.

The final element that will sustain a defeated mind is what the Holy Spirit calls the Zacchaeus Syndrome. According to the New Testament, there was a man known as Zacchaeus who was too short to see Jesus Christ as He was passing by on the road. Therefore, he decided to climb a Sycamore tree to be able to see Jesus, and he was able to get Jesus' attention. This is an awesome picture of a defeated mind and a defeated person. A defeated mind, like Zacchaeus, is too short to see past its own failures. When people do not realize that today's mistakes do not have to ruin tomorrow's future, they might just allow present failures to cancel out future successes. The defeated mind loves this kind of atmosphere. Many people never plan for the future or even have future goals because they believe that, based on their present vision, they have no true future. Since their present situation appears to be going badly whether on their jobs, in their businesses, or at school, they have already given up on securing any future place around the table of victory. Their shortsightedness has clouded any longterm vision they could have experienced. Yes, Zacchaeus was too short to see Jesus Christ, the only one who could bring him deliverance from his shame and pain, so he climbed a tree to help his sight. Some of us see ourselves as too small because our visions are too small. Then, there are those of us who can't see how God sees us because our vision is too focused on earth and not on heaven. We are so busy with our heads in the sand like ostriches that we are not able to see like eagles. The Zacchaeus Syndrome is found when future possibilities are too far out of reach for a shortsighted and defeated mind. Please remember, if you are unable to see yourself being it or doing it, then you most definitely will never possess it.

Chapter Six

Unseen Things: The Most Dangerous Things to a God-Destined Life

It is safe to say that many people fall and get injured because of unseen objects positioned right in front of them. In fact, walking through this world is like walking through a dark room with all sorts of potentially dangerous objects that Jesus Christ had to endure so that we might possess His light and be guided safely by Jesus' light through it. You might think that the worst enemies of your God-destined life are those we can see. You might even go so far as to believe that physical terrorists, guns, robbers, and invading armies might be some of the greatest threats to your safety. However, I wish to inform you that the most dangerous enemies are those which you cannot see with human eyes. In fact, the worst enemy that any army can fight is an unseen one. Think about it! How do you fight something you cannot see? This would be an impossible feat. Not knowing who, where, or what an enemy is would render even the most skilled, ready, and perfectly equipped army useless. Therefore, what I cannot see becomes the most dangerous thing to me!

This is the case in which we find ourselves. We are fighting things which are hidden from physical eyes. As a matter of fact, the Bible informs us that we are not fighting against flesh and blood, but we are waging a war over our God-transmitted faith against Satan and his demonic army. However, as if this were not bad enough, we are also in a fight against hidden spiritual terrorists within our own decaying flesh, known as works of the flesh. Yes, indeed! We have a spiritual enemy on the outside of us as well as a spiritual enemy on the inside of us. By spiritual, I am speaking about something that does not have a physical body nor can it be held or touched by physical hands. These spiritual enemies, which God instructs a believer to become equipped to fight, were around long before that believer was even born. So, while we are busy concentrating on people who talk badly about us or that coworker who is always spreading false rumors about us, we are simply being distracted from the real fight and subsequent dangers of the hidden things. You must realize that this is exactly what Satan wants us to do! Satan allows decoys to enter our lives through the front door. Then, while we lose focus of the real fight, he can easily blow our destiny sky high. We must keep our true sight (the ability to discern spiritual matters by God's spiritual Word and His Holy Spirit), focused on the hidden demonic world, as well as works of fleshy lusts hidden right beneath our skin.

I wish for you to know that our fight with Satan and his demonic clans occurred the instant we were marked by the blood of Jesus Christ and received His new Spirit life on the inside of us. Once this happened, every greasy and slimy demon was placed on red alert. Satan will not just sit back and watch potential threats to his sinful kingdom order run around worshipping and witnessing freely. Therefore, all believers, whether they know it or not, have been assigned a demonic presence with the intention of breaking their faith in God and thus ruining their witness. Please understand that the best way to convince the sinful world that there is no God would be to destroy all of the tangible evidence seeking to prove that He is real and that He has always been God. Thus, since every Christian is that touchable and real evidence of God's existence, His salvation, His power, and His deep love for all humankind, Satan is trying to kill, hide, oppress, repossess, and imprison every true born-again Christian on the planet.

Satan's first strategy is to cause Christians to downplay God's awesome future for them by getting them to doubt their value due to past sins and failures. He knows that if he wishes to silence our good witness, then he must get us to believe that we have no good witness. To cause us to believe that we have no good witness, he shows us clips of our sinful past. Believe it or not, many Christians have hidden their testimonies from their families and this world because they think that all the world and their families will see is that former drug dealer, addict, sexually promiscuous, or depressed individual. What they might not yet realize is that these are the exact realities that reveal the wonderful existence of a life-changing God. Oh, yes, our past sins act as a present testament to God's great power to deliver anyone from any kind of dark and nasty sin. Thus, our past cursed lives, when touched by the saving hands of a never-failing God can become the *very* touchable witness that God is, undeniably, who He says that He is.

Now, when getting believers to hide their present witness of God because of past sins is not effective enough, then Satan whips out another weapon. The next weapon which Satan has effectively used over the many years against Christians is the intimidation factor. If he cannot shut them up, the next and most obvious step would be to scare them quiet. That inner voice telling you that you are going nowhere in God, that God has left you, that you will never escape your momma's cancer, or that you will die at age thirty just like your daddy is nothing but the spirit of fear. This spirit is designed to cripple and torment you in such a way that you never even want to get out of bed. Fear is one of the most traumatizing weapons in Satan's arsenal. Through the operation of fear, Satan has caused so many people to commit suicide, murder someone else, and even lose their own minds. This heavy and unseen weapon is fired at the believer to stop that believer's praise, prayer, worship, and evangelistic life. If Satan can get us so afraid of the things that are outside of our homes, then maybe we won't even want to leave them. Satan causes an increase of crimes, such as murder, gang violence, robbery, and rape to increase in our neighborhoods for this very reason. All of this darkness is designed to terrify us and cause us to hide even from the face of our God. Then, while the church is so busy hiding from these atrocities, Satan continues to kill, steal, and destroy the potential of our young people. This gives him free reign to multiply ungodly abortions, increase sexually transmitted diseases such as AIDS, and totally damn nations to a Christless hell. We cannot stand for Jesus and live in fear at the same time. We cannot believe in the full power of God and be overwhelmed by the lesser power of fear, both at the same time. Something has got to go, and it most definitely must be fear!

Just in case the fear factor does not work, Satan sends in the dirt factor. Think about it! If you wanted to mess up a Christian's witness, wouldn't you simply get some kind of dirt on that person? Oh, yes, you would! One of the quickest ways to discredit people is to catch them in a moment of indiscretion or sin. In fact, one of the reasons for the fall of great preachers, politicians, or other influential people is an immoral or sinful act caught on tape or witnessed by another person. Therefore, in order to discredit the righteousness of a righteous person, catch that person performing an ungodly act. Thus, Christians everywhere must be careful and holy because Satan will do anything to put dirt on the washed garments of the Lord's righteousness upon them. Satan will send demonic spirits designed to inflame past feelings of lust to push Christians over the edge of the cliffs of fornication, adultery, pornography, or even rape. I wish to encourage you to pray, fast, run, take cold showers, love your own wife or husband, or read the Bible; just please find whatever spiritual practice it takes in order to live above ground. You must live above the mudslinging sin of Satan and his demonic host. If Satan cannot get you dirty, then everyone around you will see the purity of God's nature within you; then they themselves might want to be cleansed by His Son's precious blood!

Rest assured that Satan is a relentless enemy. He never stops fighting until his objectives are accomplished. Therefore, every Christian must resolve within themselves to be very persistent in this spiritual battle. If Satan does not win by using the dirt factor, then he will surely resort to the smear campaign, which is the use of lies, propaganda, and gossip. If he cannot find real dirt on people, then he will make some up and smear it all over their good name or God-destined life. This plan has worked to perfection for many years because even people within the church have become lovers of gossip and mudslinging. Satan knows that even we as Christians are quick to accept as truth anything said or spoken about our fellow brethren. When you find people who are quick to believe whatever is said about others, then you will always be able to smear and pervert the innocent's character and name. When Satan cannot find any evidence that you are living a sinful and defiled life, then he resorts to influencing people, who do not even truly know you, to lie about you. Once he gets enough people to hear enough lies, Satan believes this will ruin your name and, most important, your God-birthed witness. Thus, once he ruins your ability to witness about your God, he knows that people will use this as an opportunity to claim that there is really no God. Smear campaigns have worked in politics, and, much worse than politics, they have worked in Christ's church in the realm of the Christian saints. How utterly disgraceful! We have helped the enemy kill our own fellow saints by listening to lies which have never been proven to be true. This disgusting practice must end with us because it will surely not end with Satan!

Well, after all this fighting, if Satan still cannot score his desired victory, he will bring out the big gun called the counterfeit factor-If you can't beat them, join them. The New Testament reveals to us that Satan will, at times, change himself into an image of light (goodness) to infiltrate the church and confuse people as to what is really of God or what is really of him. So far, this has also worked. Satan has raised up so many religions and cults in the world that people are confused about what to believe and which is the true faith to follow. This is an awesome war tactic; if you can convince an opposing army that its own troops are the enemy, then they will begin to shoot their own soldiers, putting you in a stronger position to finish the job. This is exactly what Satan has done. By causing us to split even the true church of Jesus into many divided organizations, Satan has deceived Christians into believing that because they are Baptist, they cannot really fellowship with Pentecostals. Also, he has Anglicans believing that they are more correct concerning biblical doctrine than Methodists. We have caused so much division within the church, that it has even confused sinners. Now sinners are wondering how we can ask them to believe in our one God if we are living as if there are more than one. They will never believe if we do not live as Christ, live in His love, and live as one! Until this happens, millions are going to hell because Satan has used many of Jesus' own leaders and disciples to distract the world from the only true God that can save them. In addition, Satan has placed preachers in the church of Jesus Christ who are nothing but wolves in sheep's clothing. They sound like they belong to Jesus, dress like they belong to Jesus, preach like they belong to Jesus, and even testify that they belong to Jesus. However, behind the scenes, they are involved in vile acts, such as having sex with the single members, watching pornographic movies, having sex with underage children, stealing church funds, committing fraudulent acts, or engaging in homosexual acts. These leaders, and even fake followers, are hindering Christ's witness with their gutter-like behavior. They have caused many others in the church to lose respect for preaching and even for Christian values. You see, Satan knows that the best way to destroy a movement is from within and not from without. Sadly enough for some believers, they never saw it coming. When something looks like us, we tend not to view it as a threat to us, and we allow it to operate freely among us. However, this has caused many to backslide and walk once again in a lifestyle filled with dark and dirty practices. We have been hoodwinked! In fact, many of us are no longer able to discern truth from lies, and we are quick to follow anyone who will preach us happy and only say the things that justify our sinful actions. I believe that it is at the point now that for every true preacher called and sent by Jesus Christ to His church, there are ten fake ones being ordained; and for every truly born-again saint coming to join the church, there are ten devils already on the church's membership. We must defeat this strategy! We must learn to discern and uncover these fakes and then escort them to the door! It is time for the true army of the Lord to arise and cast out every counterfeit soldier among us!

Surely you do not think that our fight with the dangerous, hidden things stops at Satan. Oh, no! There is a fight with an enemy closer to home. This hidden and unclean enemy is called works of the flesh. The works of the flesh are all the many terrible sins in the sin nature that are locked away in the mind, emotions, and will of a sinful soul and enclosed in a very sensual and sin-driven body. You should by now know that before you were born of God's pure Spirit, you were once dead and buried in Adam and Eve's impure flesh. The sin, and ability to sin, was passed onto us through our generational bloodline from Adam and Eve. Thus, we inherited an ability to do wrong directly at birth. Even after receiving a new, living, inner spirit from God, we still have to fight with the old, decaying image of Adam and Eve known as the flesh. This fight is an ongoing one and will only cease once Jesus Christ returns and changes our human bodies into spirit-formed ones. Until then, as we await this glorious transformation of our ungodly bodies, we must prepare to face the evil that hides deep in the caves of our flesh.

According to the biblical letter of Galatians in chapter five, the Holy Spirit reveals through the apostle Paul the many types of sin terrorists that will try to penetrate our spirit life and infect it with poisonous sin toxins. The first sin seed discussed is adultery. This is when a person is having sexual relations with another person's spouse or is cheating on his or her own spouse. Married saints must be very careful in this area. Satan is always looking for some weakness in a marriage-a weak spousal link. If the two do not live always seeking to become one flesh, then they will surely become three, by adding another person into the mix who is not a spouse. Adultery wounds and breaks a mate and can leave a close-knit family in tattered pieces. This sin can destroy a pastor's ministry; if a person cannot be faithful to his or her spouse, then how can he or she truly be faithful to God. The sin of adultery is an ugly beast, and, once let out of its cage, it will try to destroy both of those involved.

Next, the letter discusses fornication, which is sexual activity performed without God's official license of marriage. Let us face reality; we live in a very sexual world! Everywhere that you turn you can find sexy outfits, sex stores, commercials filled with sexual images, and magazine's filled with sexually explicit material. Young people today are so fascinated by it that they are engaged in it at ten years of age and up. Instead of chasing God, working toward goals, striving for excellence, and trying to change a generation gone wild, millions are more interested in their next sex partner. This sin has also found its way into the church. Even many Christians engage in sex before marriage; some try to justify it by saying that they must taste the milk before they invest in the cow. Violating God's kingdom order may lead to children who lack the complete protection of a true covenant family-one in which both the father and mother have invested complete love into one another in the state of marital communion. You see, if you do not have true commitment and complete investment, then you will only aid in birthing a generation which cannot truly respect that a life should be loved and protected, not used and abused. When we use people for sex, we are teaching the generation after us that people are just fun toys. Use them today and get another one tomorrow! No wonder the world is such a cold and abusive place. We taught a generation how to be this way!

As we look further into this letter of Paul's, we find that he also writes about the sins of uncleanness and lasciviousness (outrageous behavior). These are two sins cut from the same cloth. Uncleanness is speaking about any kind of nasty act, such as pornography or homosexuality and lesbianism. These unclean acts are also considered outrageous behavior. God designed one man for one woman and one woman for one man. However, after Adam and Eve sinned, humankind began to define the kinds of relationships that they felt comfortable with and believed to be right. However, according to God's biblical standards, there is nothing right about a person watching other people have sex, or two of the same sex performing sexual acts upon each other. Oh, no! God created a man and a woman to come together in the union of marriage and only be fascinated with their own sexuality and bodies. I do not believe that there exists a gay gene because this would indirectly imply that God makes mistakes in His creation.

And, we know that He most definitely does not! A person with gay tendencies is not dealing with a gay gene, but a sinful and broken soul that is free to either choose a gay lifestyle or to cry out to God and choose a godly lifestyle.

One of the reasons rape is so prevalent is because societies have permitted such unclean behavior that a generation of twisted and sexually addicted people have now been formed. They are so sex-crazed that if they cannot get it by permission, they will get it by force. What a mess!

By now you can see just how dangerous the hidden things of our flesh are. Another sin in our flesh is idolatry, which is replacing God's presence in our lives with the presence of things. Face it! Many people love their cars, houses, spouses, and money more than they love the God who they claim has given them these blessings. Idolatry has so overtaken many of us in the church that we care more about using the gospel of Jesus to build our own names, megachurches, and conferences designed to celebrate flesh rather than God. If Paul were alive today, he would cast out many leaders who have been lifted into the place of Jesus. This is why we see very little of the true power of God now. He will never share the attention of His church. He is a very jealous God! He wants to be first in everything that we seek or desire. If He cannot be first and given our first priority and attention, then He will be gone. Our own idolatry is pushing our own God away!

As we progress, we find the sin of witchcraft very prevalent in the world and in the church. Witchcraft is not only the calling and manipulation of demons through the art of black or white magic, it is also the mixing of light and darkness.

When we as the church mix right living with works of evil, no matter how small those works might be, we are involved in a level of witchcraft. In fact, according to the Bible, any act of rebellion against God is like the sin of witchcraft. The practice of witchcraft involves talking to the dead, putting curses on people, and consulting psychics or astrology to know the future. There are many believers involved in this type of witchcraft. They attend church fellowship on Sunday, and on Monday they call some psychic hotline seeking answers that they should receive from God alone. This is wrong on so many levels. If we believe God has all the answers that we need to navigate through this maze of life, then why would we go to a witch doctor or psychic for these answers? Never go to a lesser witch when you have a greater God!

Next, there are the nasty flesh operations of hatred, variance (loving to fight), emulations (anger over not receiving one's own way), wrath (heated and passionate anger), and strife (violence). These are all sister sins, and they feed off each other. Hatred causes fights which occur because someone is trying to get his or her own way. Then, wrath takes place because of this selfish desire for people to have their own way, which generally leads to strife or violence. These are the sins that foster racial prejudice, racial profiling by police officers, racial tensions, and in the final analysis, racial division. So many people are being killed simply because someone wanted to have his or her own way. Our world is so full of angry and hateful people that if it were a balloon, it would be just about to pop. If you say a certain word in some communities or wear a particular color in others, you just might lose your life. Unfortunately, even the church has not yet put these operations of the flesh in their graves. Some of us are just as hotheaded as those in the world. We have church business meetings that end in all-out brawls. You would think that we were having a yelling match when you look at how we handle some of the business of Christ's church. There was a time when there was so much love and tolerance within the church that you would hardly find an argument. However, now we have replaced peaceful gatherings with drive-by shooting meetings. These sins are tearing us apart from within, and Satan is laughing at us from without. Hollywood is making comedic movies about how we as church people behave. They laugh at how we, who claim to be peacemakers, are acting just as violent as their movies we preach against. How hypocritical of us! By the powerful character of God in our spirits, we must restore the true image which Christ Himself gave to us.

The next flesh sin on the list is seditions. This word means division or disunion. If you were to look at the church today, you would have to confess that we are more divided now than ever. Many assumed that by creating all these denominations, we would be gathering the body together. The problem with this theory is that, although these denominations have truly gathered saints together, they have done so only unto each separate group. Thus, we are no longer grouped as the church of Jesus, one church; instead, we are groups of Baptist, Pentecostal, Methodist, Church of God, etc. Instead of recognizing that we were all washed in one blood and baptized into one body, we view each other based on our differences and not our similarities. The church has become so divided that some people believe that if you are not a part of their denomination, you are on your way to hell. It has gotten to the point that some pastors will never call on a pastor from another denomination to preach at his denomination's revival.

When we are split like this, we will never truly be whole. We will only ever have half of the puzzle which the Holy Ghost's grace has allowed us to put together. If we will not completely join as one body and no longer be separated as many denominational bodies, then we will never truly see the fullness of the entire kingdom of God. It takes all of the parts to reveal all of Jesus Christ, our head, to the entire body of Christ. And, there is not one of us nor one denomination that can boast of having the full and entire revelation of God! Not one!

As we move along, take a look at this nasty sin called heresy. The word heresy describes opinioned lies designed to convince people that there is no God, hell, or judgment, and that good deeds will get a person into heaven. This sin in the flesh is exactly why atheism exists. Heresy is found in the mind that has already deceived itself. A person who has allowed this inner sin to take up residence has already blocked any witness of God or the conviction of the Holy Spirit from persuading it. This sin is born when a skeptical mind connects with very skeptical words and then allows the marriage of the two. In fact, spiritually speaking, when a skeptic (one who is suspicious about everything) and a heretic (one who is filled with opinionated lies) come together, they give birth to an atheist (one who does not accept the reality of God). Heresies are so very dangerous, and once they are given the slightest bit of belief space, they will rapidly take over any mind and turn it from any truth it might have been taught. Heresy is like an aggressive from of cancer; it eats away every bit of truth until falsehood is all that remains.

Are you sober yet? Well, based on the evidence presented thus far, you should be very awake and spiritually alert! We are not done yet, so keep paying close attention to the other sin seeds hidden deep within our flesh. The written letter of Galatians then informs us of envy. This is an intense dislike for someone because he or she has something that the envious person does not. This sin has caused children to kill others kids for tennis shoes. A little envy has caused a man to kill another man in order to get his car, house, or even his wife. This is the sin that keeps adding more sins to itself. In fact, envy can lead to hatred, and hatred can lead to murder. We have got to be thankful for all that God has given us or we will end up envious of what others have been blessed with. Envy might lead us to spread false rumors about how they got that blessing or even attempt to steal it from them. Believe me when I tell you, this is not the kind of hidden sin that you or I would want to take for granted and not deal with as soon as it rears its ugly head. Therefore, if it is not yours, do not spend time thinking about it. Thinking about it, even for a moment, might cause you to become envious of the owner.

Finally, the letter to the Galatians informs us about the sins of murder, drunkenness, and revelings (loose living). Murder is final. When a life is taken from this earth, because of this sin, it is gone from this earth completely. When we think of murder, we usually picture someone killing someone else with some sort of weapon. Although this is true, there are other ways in which a person can be murdered. We can kill a person's good name by lies and gossip, or we could slaughter a person's good character by false accusations. I do believe that there are some Christians who have become excellent and very deadly assassins, skilled in the art of destroying people by destroying their good name. This kind of behavior is ungodly and so destructive that it has caused church fellowships to crumble. It has caused husbands to leave their innocent wives and wives to leave their innocent husbands. Unlike physical death in which a victim is no longer aware of this present world, the person whose character has been assassinated has to live with his or her name being lambasted and drug through the mud. This is a very difficult to endure!

Now let us look at drunkenness. Drunkenness is not just about intoxication from strong wine or liquor; it is also dealing with all kinds of addictions. Within our bodies, there lives a soul that can become very addicted. When the human mind becomes stimulated by what the body sees, tastes, touches, or smells, it develops a memory at that very moment. If it liked what it was introduced to, it will constantly ask the body to take that substance into itself again. It is at this very moment that the mind and the body's appetite is becoming addicted to that substance. Therefore, the more the human body experiences any substance, the more the brain wants to experience the sensation derived from it. Once this happens, it becomes harder and harder for the brain and the body to do without a particular substance. Some addictions are not as bad as others, but all will lead to a dependency that should only be transferred to God. We must begin to break even the good addictions. The only thing that we should be addicted to is our God!

Then we come to revelings or loose living. I believe that this sums up all possible types of sin without mentioning them one by one. Many Christians are living just as loose as sinners of this world system. In this kind of lifestyle, anything goes. There are no limits nor boundaries. If you want someone's wife or husband, just do it. If you want to have sex with a perfect stranger, just do it. This kind of lifestyle doesn't care for the victims it leaves in its wake; it just wants to do what feels good. God can never rule in a life like this, which is why this kind of behavior is so dangerous. If God cannot rule it, He is not going to protect it. This is why many single Christians are contracting AIDS and other STDs today. They want to live loosely, have multiple sexual partners, and pray to God to protect them from any sexually transmitted disease. It does not work this way! What we sow in this life, we are going to reap. Not even God can alter this principle or rule. If we live an ungodly life, then we are living a truly unprotected life!

Now, in the light of all this information, do you still believe that the most dangerous things are the physical and visible things around you? I think not. The things that we should be most concerned about are not the things that go bump in the night, but the things which never go bump at all. It's the unseen things that make the most impact in our God-destined lives, if we should leave them unchecked. We must master these satanic movers and these flesh operations by walking in obedience to God's Word, His Spirit's leading, and His kingdom's rules. By the power of God and the demonstration of His Holy Ghost, you can rise above every hidden thing, whether satanic or fleshy.

CHAPTER SEVEN

THE BIGGER THE GIANT, THE GREATER THE DESTINY

EVERY LIFE THAT has been destined by God for a great use or purpose will soon discover that the greatness of the destiny determines the size of the giant to be faced. Now I realize that we are not usually comfortable with the notion that to be greatly used by God, we must endure great mountains of setbacks, hindrances, failures, and agonies. However, this is the path which prepares the greatest of God's chosen warriors. Please understand that the path of the greatest resistance is necessary for the greatest release of God's power and might through any vessel. Therefore, if we are afraid of giants, then we are truly afraid of the possibility of a great destiny. There is no great destiny in God that is giant free. In fact, every man or woman in the Bible who was used mightily by God had to face enormous giants. Whether these giants were real or figurative, they had to be faced nonetheless. I will venture so far as to inform you that if you do not accept the giants as part of a potentially great destiny, then you will forfeit that destiny to another vessel who will gladly face the giant's test. Giants are signs to us of how big or enormous the work and will of God is within our lives. Thus, the bigger the giant, the greater the destiny.

Destiny represents a specific task that we are meant to do in a specific time or a certain place and moment in which we are supposed to exist. For every human being ever born, God has written a script of His destiny for their own lives. Although this is wonderful and perfect, one must also realize that Satan also has written a competing and deadly script for the lives of every human on the planet. This is where the giants are fashioned. God allows Satan to form the giants that will fight for his diabolical script to be accomplished. Satan wishes to place us under demonic house arrest, while using our very existence to finish the evil works he began the very moment that he fought against his own God and then deceived Adam and Eve-God's human creations. On the other hand, God has designed that every person on this earth come to know Jesus Christ, become true worshippers of Him, receive the power of His Holy Ghost, and then reach every lost sinner with the power of His gospel. God wants a dedicated people to manifest His face on this earth, but Satan wants to twist that destiny and get those same people to manifest his ugly face to the nations of this world.

If you are truly God's child and are maturing in Him, then I wish to inform you that there is a giant you must face for every level of growth that you will accomplish. In natural life this rule is obvious. The older a person gets, the more respon sibility he or she is given. This is just the way of nature and life. Therefore, the more anointed, matured, and faithful you become in God, the more giants you will face and experience. Sometimes, you and I will think that it is unfair for God to put ten tons onto our backs, while other believers are barely given five pounds. If you have been called by God to perform great acts on His behalf, there are likely to be many days that you will literally shake your fists in the air at your God because of the heaviness of the weights that He has chosen for you to lift. Listen, in these moments, when it feels like you are about to lose your mind, your lunch, and maybe even your life, remember that God does not allow spiritual wimps to fight against heavyweight giant contenders. He sends his best in order to face the best of a giant experience. Now, I know that sometimes, because of our own rebellion, we cause giants to fight against us. In this case, we usually lose, because our own sins have weakened our ability to stand against those giants. However, when we face giants because of a strong and spiritual walk with God, in His destiny for us, then we will be able to release such a knockout blow to them that it will be heard around the demonic world.

Giants are born in order to be faced. God intends for those with great destinies in Him to meet the challenge of facing giants on a daily basis. Before God releases any preacher or believer to be an effective witness for Him, He first allows Satan to prepare the right giant for that individual. God believes in running complete tests on any vessel that He has manufactured before it is allowed into the showroom of earth. There is no good or sensible manufacturer of vehicles that would send any vehicle to a showroom without running every possible safety test. If this manufacturer sent out untested vehicles and someone were to get injured, that manufacturer would be held completely responsible for all damages. Our God is not in the business of sending untested, ill-prepared, or unskilled ministry workers out into the fields of harvest. The job of ministry is too vital for Him to do that. One of the reasons there are weak-minded and non-spiritual leaders in today's church is because men and women, who have never been tried in the fires of testing or have never faced the giants of godly character building, have been ordained by other leaders and quickly sent out to do the work of ministries for which they were not prepared. Although some of these so-called leaders might have been called, many of them were not anointed (Holy Spirit authorized or activated), and others of them have not been made giant-proof or character-tested. It is very dangerous to unleash on this world leaders who have not been proven to have renounced the pleasures of it and who have never faced nor defeated one giant within it. Even David, in the Old Testament, told King Saul that he would not use his armor since he had never tested it. What this sinful world and the sainted church need are giant-tested warriors of God!

You and I need giants to test us and enable us to recognize where we are strong or weak, whether or not we are maturing, if we are ready for God's great destiny or not, or even ready to hold the armor of someone who is ready. Giants then help us gauge our truest standing in the kingdom of God and in the world of humankind. Therefore, we need giants as much as we need the breath of God's Holy Spirit. Oh, yes! We cannot really live without them!

As we face the giants of this satanic world order, please be advised that these obstacles are also Satan's strategic weapons, unleashed against us to sabotage every God- appointed destiny planned by God for us. These giants are not to be toyed with and neither are they going to play games with us. These giants arc dangcrously clever, deceptive, and strong vices with which we have to deal.

There is really no need for you to fear the giants which God allows, seeing that these giants are not designed to kill the God-design in you but are purposed to kill the sinful design of human, fleshy frailty. In an awesome sense, your giants will be more of a benefit to you than a best friend or parent ever could. Once again, in order for you to reach the becoming stage of God's destiny for your life, you must be undone and remade by every giant test which God sends your way. You cannot walk in the fullness of all that is Jesus Christ if you are too afraid to first walk with your giants. Please understand that God is not in the business of making wimps! However, He is most certainly in the business of forging warriors. A wimp can be formed in one day but will never last one minute in this world of satanic darkness. A warrior, on the other hand, takes a lifetime to be forged but will endure for all eternity and shall reign victoriously with God. So, here is the fundamental question: "Would you rather be a wimp or a warrior?" If your answer to this soul-searching question is that you would prefer to become a warrior, then my humble suggestion is to face every God-sent giant and ask God for more. The more giants you face will determine the kind of warrior you will become. Face them all!

Well, let us say that you have decided to accept your trial by giant. You have decided before God that you want to begin giant boot camp, and you are ready to begin with heaven's tactical training and conditioning of your mind and your spirit. While you are ready and psyched for the challenges that await you, you have this nagging thought in the back of your mind, "I wonder what my first giant will be?" Just as your mind is quietly thinking this very important thought, God sends a memo directly into your spirit informing you that you are already facing your first giant. You never even noticed he was there. In great amazement, you wonder *My first giant has already been here, and I did not know it?* As you stand with a confused look on your face, your heavenly Father says that you are actually staring in the giant's face right now, and the giant is the reality that you are alone. The feeling you have felt for days now, and the companions who no longer wish to be around you, are the symptoms of the giant called loneliness. Whenever God prepares any vessel for a great ministry of great impact on the lives of men and women, the first thing He does is to unleash the giant of alone. One example of this is when God was calling Moses to be a great leader and deliver God's people. God removed Moses from Pharaoh's house and Egypt. God caused Moses to come alone to a mountain where only he and God were present. No one can ever become what God has intended and do what God has willed unless he or she is separated by the giant of being alone. When a person is taken to the alone place with God, God begins to break all distractions and change mindsets. God takes the fearfulness, doubt, and insecurity away from a vessel in the alone place by removing people who have helped condition this person's mind to be fearful, doubtful, and insecure. Although this all sounds very good and wonderful, this is one of the hardest test experiences any of us will ever face. Being conditioned alone with God is so difficult because, as human beings, we were made to be social creatures. Think about it. It took two human beings, intimately joined together in a sexual embrace, to cause us to be conceived. Then, we were nurtured by the intimate connection of an umbilical cord, which kept us socially attached to the mother who carried us for nine months. Then, as if this were not enough human bonding, we were brought up in a family, wherein we were usually in the presence of a brother, sister, aunt, cousin, or grandparent. We might as well face reality; we were not conceived alone, birthed alone, nor were we ever made to be alone. Therefore, in order for God to have us all to Himself, so that we learn to trust Him more than the families into which we were born, He has to strip them away from us for a season. It is during this season of loneliness testing that we learn to believe what God says more than what people will say. As we face and stare down this giant, although we are caught in the pains of loneliness, we will begin to grow so intimately and strongly dependent upon God that if people walk out on us while we are in the ministry, we will never retreat nor surrender. You see, God is making you like solid iron-unbreakable. When you have faced this giant of alone, you will never be broken into pieces by the lies, doubts, or the condemning words from jealous folk. When Jesus Christ was about to perform the greatest work known to humankind, the work of salvation, God brought him to the Garden of Gethsemane, and his disciples left him alone and fell asleep. They could not even pray with him a short moment. Jesus felt the pains of being rejected by his own and being alone. While on His cross, the Bible reveals to us that the heavens became as black as pitch, and Jesus asked His heavenly Father why He was being forsaken. By the revelation of the Holy Ghost, I believe that Jesus did not really believe that His Father had forsaken Him, instead He wanted us to realize that at times we are going to feel as if God has left us all alone. Thus, this is a valuable lesson that we must keep deep in the crevasses of our minds. If Jesus Christ, the very Son of God, experienced this feeling in His flesh, then so will we. Whether we like it or not, we are going to walk through the valley of loneliness if we are to become all that God wants us to be. Please realize that strong kingdom leaders are developed when God causes them to be alone. Anybody can act tough and strong when in a crowd or in a gang, but not everybody can truly stand strong and stand alone. When I was being formed as an apostle of Jesus Christ, there was a time in my single life that God had me so wrapped up in Him that I had no desire to be with a girlfriend. I had some Christian friends who were dating and seeking relationships with the opposite sex, but I was too busy studying the Bible, praying, fasting, and attending church fellowship. Believe it or not, I was considered strange. Only those who have placed their own pleasures and passions in front of a passionate and intimate longing for God would think this way. Well, I did not care. I continued to stay in the alone place, gathering knowledge of my God and learning how to be led by His Holy Spirit. Now, I am so glad that I faced this giant that others ran away from, because I have so much revelation from God and about God which I intend, by His power, to release to the body of Christ. I want to pour out all of this Holy Spirit manifestation of power upon all who are hungry for the next great move of God. And, I am not the only one God wants to use in this way. If you will not allow God to do the same with your life, then millions could miss out on the revelation and power of God destined to flow from the Holy Ghost through you. Remember that there is no relationship as good or even better than an intimate joining with God in Christ Jesus. There is no husband or wife, father or mother, girlfriend or boyfriend that can ever equal the blissful experience that awaits us in God. Husbands and wives might leave us; mothers or fathers might die before us; and girlfriends and boyfriends could reject us, but God will always be with us. You cannot beat this offer even if you had a billion dollars! Therefore, allow the giant of the alone experience to carry you far away, until you are so lost in God that you would not care to be found!

Wow! With all this nail-biting giant adventure awaiting you, you are probably excited to discover the face of your next giant. The next giant you will rneet is what the Holy Spirit calls the giant of the Gideon experience, which says numbers do not really matter. To further recognize and know about this giant, it would be helpful to know a little bit about the man known as Gideon. Gideon was an Old Testament biblical man of God, who was chosen by God to lead the children of Israel in war against the huge, combined armies of the Midianites, Amalekites, and the children of the East. Well, the biblical story reveals that at first Gideon had more than ten thousand fighting men-an army already too small to war against their countless enemies. However, God then commanded Gideon to cut his already depleted and small band of soldiers down to three hundred men. I believe if you or I were asked by God to do what seemed to be very crazy and suicidal, I would have probably cursed the heavens for allowing me to have been born. However, Gideon was not so foolish. He did what God required of him, and his little army, with its very big God, crushed their enemies and won what had appeared to be a very impossible battle. This is a beautiful lesson for those of us who aspire to lead God's troops into battle against the hordes of Satanic lead demons. The lesson here is that God does not win great battles with great numbers. He is all-powerful alone, and He does not need the puny strength of huge numbers of clay humankind to secure complete victory. Therefore, if you are going to be used by God in this great spiritual warfare, then you are going to be trained and processed by the giant of the Gideon experience. There is no way around this reality. Anyone can feel competent and encouraged to lead an army into battle if he or she has a million soldiers. I mean, who in their right mind would not want to lead a church, psalmist team, deacon board, or evangelistic rnission boasting these kinds of numbers? In the church of Jesus Christ today, we as believers have been making huge egotistical boastings about which pastor has the largest congregation, which televangelist has the greatest show ratings, which gospel singer has sold the most records, which preacher is considered the best or one of the top twenty preachers of the twenty-first century, and which churches are the megachurches around the world. Someone should have told us that this kind of boasting is not only ridiculous, but it is also idolatrous. We have begun to place our trust in the numbers and the strength of people more than in the very God whom we claim to love above all others. Many Christians today have believed the words of singers, preachers, and modern-day philosophers just because they have large churches, great music, and large followings. These believers have been so moved by these little vessels of clay that they are no longer able to be moved by the Spirit of God. This is why God wanted Gideon to have the smallest number of people as he went into battle. At the end of the battle, God did not want Gideon nor the nation of Israel to believe that it was by their numbers or their strength that the battle was won. God wanted to get the praise and glory alone! God is the only being who truly deserves the praise and the glory all by Himself! Before God decides to use us, he must ensure that we are comfortable and confident with small numbers, small experiences, and small help. If you are a truly called apostle, pastor, evangelist, prophet, or teacher, do not be afraid of small numbers nor small beginnings. This is the experience with which God creates great life-changing leaders. Think about it! Jesus started with the twelve, and He has done such great works that even preachers in this day, who have millions of followers worldwide, have not been able to fully duplicate all of the miraculous works that Jesus has done. Jesus had no access to electricity or television studios, yet He was still able to touch this entire world with His divine presence. How about that for not needing great numbers or great anything? God is the greatness that you need! Do not be afraid of the giant of the Gideon experience because with God, numbers, size, physical power, human advantage, social connections, and physical wealth access do not and never will matter. God can take a person with five cents and give him or her a television ministry worth five million dollars, without the aid of social connections. Instead of trying to get into the right network of Christian leaders or business owners, simply trust God as your only true connection, and watch Him cause you to go farther and possess more capital than you ever thought possible. Once you have proven that you can face the challenge of this Gideon experience, then you would have opened yourself up to God in such a manner that He would give you a large corporation, starting with just one employee and an overdrawn business account. God can cause you to reach your entire state of five million people with just five disciples or members. I am telling you that God will give you CEO positions, although you only possess an insignificant GED. God can perform His greatest miracles when there is the smallest group of believers. So, if you and I are going to work for our awesome God, we are going to have to shrink our huge egos and put aside our thoughts of greatness. To be truly great in the kingdom of God, you must become very small; in order to be truly strong, you must become extremely weak; in order to have great spiritual vision, you must become blind; and in order to move enormous, impossible mountains, you must simply have a small mustard seed-like faith. With God on your side, it takes very little of you to accomplish a very great spiritual movement on this earth. I wish for you to be encouraged by this truth and never forget that, with God, one person truly can be the majority.

As soon as you would have been fashioned by the painful blows of the Gideon's experience giant, you will have to tangle with another *very* unpleasant giant. This is one that is *very* shameful to experience and, in the midst of it, you may feel as if you and your entire existence mean nothing. I am referring to the giant of lack. This is the giant that brings you to a place in your walk with God, wherein you have no money, credit score, ministry, publicity, nor any name worth mentioning. This is the stage in God's processing of your life in which you are reduced to dust. During this struggle for purpose to live in you, God will allow your money to dry up and may allow the giant of lack to suck you so dry that friends and family will be ashamed to own you. Think this is bad? Well, I say to you that besides your wonderful relationship with the Most High God, this is the next best thing that could ever happen to you. In order for God to make you into something that neither your mother nor your father could have ever conceived and given birth to, He has to break you down into dust particles. God will cause everything that you place any kind of confidence in to become unable to support your life because He alone should be your sustainer. God made the first man, Adam, out of dust to reveal to us that He is capable of trans-forming negative things and horrible situations into something alive and miraculous. He also used dust to teach us that He can take the rubbish, failures, weaknesses, and poor decisions of our lives and make us vessels that are stronger than our last weakness. He will make us wiser than our last foolish choice. He can definitely make us more successful than our last failure. Therefore, if you are going to be more and do more on God's behalf than you ever thought possible, you are going to have to be dismantled and reassembled by God's mighty Spirit. Although this process is a very painful one, if you completely submit yourself to the God of it, great benefit and increase shall be yours. I must warn you, however, that people may laugh at your breaking. Even Christians, who do not understand this process of God, will talk about you as if you were a curse. Some are going to say that maybe you sinned against God or backslid. Please pay no attention to them! Do you remember the story of Job in the Old Testament? Job went through the same process of being reduced to dust. He had great wealth, animal livestock, and beautiful children. God even called him a perfect man in his generation. Although Job had all of this comfort and heavenly blessing, God was not finished working on him. God wanted him to not only face the challenges in his life and come out godly on the other side, but He also wanted Job to face Satan himself and come out victorious and still righteous on the other side. In other words, although Job was perfect, he was perfect at handling the tests of men. However, God wanted him to be perfect during and after handling the test of Satan. This is so much like our God! He is always remaking us so that we might be more than we were yesterday, and far greater in the future than we are today. Our God is seeking to bring out His best from within us. The story of Job continues as God allowed Satan to kill his children, destroy his livestock, and inflict Job's body with burning boils. Job, the most righteous and wealthiest man in his day, in a moment was reduced to nothing but dust. When Job's friends saw this, some of them quickly said that Job had sinned and even accused him of being cursed by God. Thank God the story does not end here! After Job was unmade in order to be remade, God restored all of Job's wealth and gave him more beautiful children. Then, God made those same friends return to him and beg his forgiveness so that they would not receive a curse themselves. Thus, Job is a very real example of how God can strip us bare, only to clothe us again with richer garments. Do not be so discouraged in your lack that you miss the abundance of God on the other side. The same Christians who laugh at you because your ministry only has five people, your bank account only has two dollars, or you only have two outfits in your closet may one day ask you to relieve them of their lack. If you stand in faith, walk after the leading of God's Spirit, and have cut off the head of the giant of lack, you will be used by God to free many others from their poverty, sin, depression, and fear. I want you to be assured that this giant that you must face today will help you deliver people from their problems and giants tomorrow. Fight, baby! Fight! Someone who does not possess the will to fight is depending on the God in you to help bring breakthrough.

Another giant you must face is acceptance. As human beings, we want to be accepted and treated well by others so much, that we sometimes let go of our views and convictions. This is what we know as the great compromise. Now, although some levels of compromise are good, compromise can be very bad. Before God will greatly use a vessel, He is going to make certain that that vessel is able to be taunted and laughed at without betraying His words and standards. Over the past twenty years, some preachers have put aside the real, spirit-transforming truth of God because they were afraid of losing congregations, jobs, friends, or their standing in this sinful world. In fact, those preachers who want to be friends with the sinful world have refused to preach on certain abominable sins within the cities, states, and countries in which they reside. They are afraid to touch on these touchy subjects because they don't want to lose the thousands of members and the many thousands of dollars passing through their local assemblies every Sunday. Since this action must be rebuked, God is raising up a new breed of preachers. He is blowing His awesome breath upon unknown saints who do not want to be in the back pocket of politicians or people of affluence. These saints shall become God's chosen preachers and they will preach what God wishes, even if they are rejected by family or friends. Once you prove to God that you do not care what people have to say about how you fast, pray, preach, or worship your King, then God will pour Himself so mightily upon you, that you will bring many of the world's rejects to the God who will receive them as His very own. You should also know that being accepted by people is very overrated! It is far better to be accepted by God! You are slave to no person. If you are in Jesus Christ and you belong to God, then you are His alone!

Should you be graced enough and have enough spiritual fortitude to face and overcome acceptance, then before you sigh in relief, look over your shoulder and prepare yourself for its cousin. This happens to be the giant of rejection. Many people fear rejection, and just about all human beings have had or will have a bitter taste of this terrible experience. As a rule, human beings do not like rejection, or even the thought that they may have been rejected, because we have been designed socially to be loved, nurtured, and coddled from birth. We are conditioned to want love. A baby will cling tightly to its parent, not really wanting to be held by anyone else because the baby feels that being separated from his parent is the same as being rejected. Therefore, it would appear that from birth we have been conditioned to be emotionally weak and dependent because of our need to be accepted and not rejected. In later years, some discover that they have run after the wrong relationships and held onto the wrong people because they are afraid to face any kind of rejection. If God's will is going to be fulfilled within our lives, we are going to have to learn to be numb in the face of rejection. Because the *ways* of God are so despised by the sinful world, when we open our mouths to preach against acts such as fornication, homosexuality, or that sin always results in some kind of death, we must be prepared to be despised also. Listen, even Jesus told His disciples that the sinful world would not like them because the world did not love Him. So, anything that would lead us to befriend sinners and justify their sinful ways just so we can avoid rejection is not of Jesus. Please understand that it is possible that some people on your job might be avoiding you at lunch, the water cooler, or social events because they despise you for the Christ that you represent. Do not even pay them any attention; continue to live and walk passionately with your God! Do not fear sinners or anyone else because they might reject you. You can face this giant and knock its head clean off its body!

Finally, the last giant in our list that you must face to be greatly used in the destiny of God is what the Holy Ghost calls the pause. This is by far the toughest giant with which you will have to tangle. So, get your boxing gloves on and prepare for a very long match. This giant is designed to test and try you until Jesus returns to earth for you. The one question posed by this giant is this, "Can you stand the long wait for a great destiny?" In this test, God will give you a quick prophecy concerning how great He is going to use you; then He will place you in the care of the process of waiting. God may make you wait so long for the fulfillment of the promise that you will begin to doubt whether or not God ever said it in the first place. In the Bible, when God told Abraham that the people of Israel would one day possess the land of Canaan, it took approximately four hundred years before they were led by Moses, and then Joshua, into the Land of Promise. Even when God was making the heavens and the earth as recorded in the Book of Genesis chapter 1, you will notice that between the Spirit of God hovering over the darkness in verse 2 and God actually speaking in verse 3, there is a dramatic pause. It is only after this pause that God commands light to exist. When God is creating something that has never existed before, He does not rush the making of it. He takes His time! This is one of the reasons He did not create the heavens and the earth in one day. Therefore, do not be discouraged if that ministry, house, job, husband, wife, or promotion, which God has promised you, has not yet come to pass; God is just taking His time to ensure that you have the best. Please realize that God lives outside of time, in eternity; He is not affected by time as we are. In fact, the Bible informs us that one day to God is like one thousand to us, and one thou-sand days to us is like one day to Him. This means that God is able to make our one thousand days of waiting return to us as if it were just the passing of one day. Hey, with a God like this, who cares about how long we must wait on Him? When He shows up, He is going to so fulfill our present lives that it would appear as if not even the hands on our watches or clocks have moved. God will always be on time as it pertains to what He has promised us because He is not operating on our earth-based, physical time. His clock is eternity, and eternity has no beginning or ending! God is the only being powerful enough to stop time, roll back time, and pause time to cause His destiny to come alive in our lifetime. What an awesome God! So, enjoy the pause while it lasts. The pause will allow God to grant you the greatest movement of His Holy Spirit and His holy purpose within your life. The pause is your perfection!

I do hope that by now you are in love with the reality that you have been assigned these giants. As long as you live according to the Word of God and His Spirit, you will be filled with joyous laughter as you meet every giant and watch your spirit grow within you. Therefore, say hello to your giants, today. I guarantee they will be saying hello to you.

Chapter Eight

Surviving the Lion's Den: Your Exit Strategy

THE WORLD IN which you as a believer live can be defined as one huge satanic trap. This sinful design of wicked practices, evil thinking, and wrong actions-rape, murder, hatred, violence, lies, and sexual perversions-combine to create a very toxic reality. Satan has crafted a very large lion's den, filled with hungry lions. Oh, yes, my friends. If we are not awake and spiritually discerning, this world could very easily break our faith, spirit, and our soul. So many believers have turned away from their commitments to God and turned to the pleasures of this world that many sinners believe that their sinful world is not so bad. In fact, Satan uses the back-sliding of Christians to convince sinners that his dangerous world order is very safe. However, the Christians who have not walked away from God know that Satan's world is a lion's den of terror, pain, godlessness, darkness, and judgment. These Christians fight to protect themselves from the devouring lions of lust, unholy passions, or evil thinking.

Once you realize that this world is such a nasty, devouring den of lions, then you must know that there are ways through which you can survive and make it out in good spiritual condition. Even as the biblical character Daniel was able to come out of the physical lion's den alive, so too will you be able to sleep among the lions and never become their meal. I believe that there is a kingdom of God strategy, revealed by His Holy Spirit, concerning every enemy we face. Even Satan has weaknesses just waiting to be discovered, uncovered, and defeated by a Holy Spirit-filled and holy walking Christian. Therefore, if there is a lion's den to be faced, then it can be defeated. Jesus Christ proved this very truth when he entered into the lion's den of this sinful world, put on Himself defeated human flesh, lived without ever sinning, and then took the keys of power over the souls of humankind from the devil. Jesus walked over every satanic lion known to humankind and gave the presence and power of His Holy Spirit to every born-again believer who will ask.

Your strategy in handling this lion's den of the sinful world is to first receive a different and more powerful birth, untouched by a genetic, sinful death cycle. There is no way to defeat the desire for sex before marriage, lying, stealing, and every other hungry lion of sin, if we are still carrying the birth desire for sin within our bodies. Therefore, believers who have been given a new and living spirit from God are now so filled with God's nature that they have the ability to break the teeth of sin's lions. Think about this! When you walk in a new and living way, you have an immunity from the contagious reality of sin. Although you will be tempted, just like any other sinner, you can triumph over the same lies and deceptions that would cause that sinner to fall. God's nature deep within your spirit is the heavenly power to walk over the things that once caused you to fail. Sins that once caused you to miss God's purpose and design now have no power over your mind and will no longer hinder you from doing it God's way. This is powerful stuff! Having this new, God-breathed spirit in you is your ticket into and out of every lion's den experience. If sin cannot penetrate God's image and His essence, and you are carrying God's image and essence, then is sin really a match for you? No way in heaven! You must see that God living on the inside of you is the most explosive element against sin's nuclear ability. Therefore, if sin is like a nuclear blast, then the character of God in the living spirit is the diffuser for sin's bomb. Sin cannot thrive in any life that has a greater life within it and has been given the ability to tell sin "No" and mean it. This is what the new birth of God does. It is the ability to say, "No" to sin's advances and to shut the mouths of all of sin's lions. Thus, God's character power within you does not just allow you to say no to sin, it makes you never want to say, "Yes" again. This is some serious, God-birthed influential power. You cannot go wrong when you have been reborn right. Once God has granted you this brand-new, never-seen-before life, you now possess all of heaven's help while in your lion's den. You never have to panic when you see the lions coming. Simply stand on heaven's ground, and the nature of God will take over. He will shift your eyes from sights of worldly pleasure. Your ears will only hear the sweet voice of the Holy Spirit and not the voice of that sexual woman or man. Your hands shall only want to grab the Bible and not an addictive substance. Your feet will simply bring you to your knees in prayer and not walk you into that strip bar. Finally, your mind shall be fixed on the things of God and not on its own selfish desires. With God's nature ruling your body, soul, and spirit, you will never be ruled by sin's lions again. Please be aware that when you are able to walk God's way, there is no way that sin can win. If Satan is trying to cause you to fight someone who has hurt you, use the love of God and love an enemy into becoming a friend of God. When Satan is tempting you to get revenge on someone who has spoken lies against your name, don't tell lies on that person in return. Instead, pray to God that this person will be delivered from a lying tongue. Live according to the new you and not the old you because someone else is being devoured by the lion's den of sin and needs to know that it is possible to make it out alive.

Your new birth is born to fight lions and win every time. It is not the only good news from heaven for you. God has also given you access to His all-powerful Spirit. Not only does God intend for you to enter the lion's den with His character, but He also wants you to enter with His manifested power. This manifested power of God is released to the believer who asks for the baptism or infilling of the Holy Spirit. You see, the character of God enables you to stand against the sin lions that roar, but the power of the active, infilling Holy Spirit enables you to deliver someone else from the jaws of the lions within that den. The power of the Holy Spirit, poured onto your life, grants you the boldness and gifts of the Holy Spirit which allow you to bring God's strength into the weakness of other saints. According to the New Testament, the gifts of the Spirit are a mixture of preaching offices and other support-flowing, Holy Spirit manifestations. With these gifts, you may have the ability to preach in such a power of God that many would be inspired to face their lions. Or, you may be able to bring

God's healing to sick bodies, resurrect dead bodies or things that have died in the lives of believers, recognize the demons at work, speak in foreign languages (tongues), be able to interpret languages without ever having trained in them, and have God's wisdom or answers for every situation requiring it. With these awesome gifts of God, sinners would see the reality of God's presence and be more quick to believe that He exists. Therefore, God also uses these gifts as signs and wonders to unbelievers around you so that they would be persuaded to come to Him for salvation. Not only does the filling of the Holy Spirit give you God's manifested power, but He will also give you the boldness to stand up for Him, even if it meant your death. This is power! The boldness to not fear death is very powerful!

Well, let us talk some more about spiritual gifts. The gifts of God's Spirit are very necessary to the church because they are used to equip believers to handle the teeth, jaws, and violence of the lions. Without these gifts, released through the baptism of the Holy Spirit, the church would not have the strength of God and would surely be too weak to handle the pressures of this satanic lion's den. In order to face a very strong demonic presence, the church must have a power far greater than it. Therefore, the only way to possess the power of God is by the baptism of the Holy Spirit, and only by the gifts of the Holy Spirit can the power of God be released in the measure necessary to shut the mouths of lions. The church needs the filling of the Holy Spirit and the gifts of the Holy Spirit if she is to survive the carnage of this satanic world's den of lions.

Walking in God's extreme power is very necessary, but it is only part of the wonderful, God-given abilities available to handle lions. If the nature of God (in the form of a reborn spirit) enables us to stand against sin and the baptism of the Holy Spirit manifests God's power (through the gifts of the Spirit), and allows us to bring deliverance to other saints, then the weapons of the Holy Spirit must make us able to stand face to face with strong demons sent to depress and possess us. According to the New Testament, we have been given God's weapons so we can remain under His control and never return to being captives of Satan's armies. Although these weapons exist within us after we have been born of the Holy Spirit, or born again, they become activated after we have been baptized in the Holy Spirit. Once these weapons are acti vated, we can use them at will to defeat any satanic plan of sabotage set against our destiny.

The first weapon allows you to have God's vision. You will be able to recognize truth from lies, light from darkness, and the real from any counterfeit. This weapon is truth. It is the ability to almost never be fooled by demons, no matter what forms or shapes they take to disguise themselves. If you could see this clearly, you would always have an advantage over every strategy of the devil. The weapon of truth is what God is and allows Him to never be wrong. Can you imagine having access to this weapon? Well, guess what? You not only have access to it, but you have been authorized by God to use it and use it well. Truth as a weapon would allow you to tell the doctor that while you may have been diagnosed with cancer, God's truth speaking to you might be telling you that the cancer was never yours and that it is no longer going to grow within you. Therefore, if this is your case, then the weapon of truth can connect you to a place in God where cancer does not, nor will it ever be able, to exist. You better walk in the weapon of truth. The truth of the matter is that in Jesus Christ, you win!

Since God is very diverse and multifaceted, you must believe that He is too big to have only one weapon. God has more weapons, tailor-made for His chosen vessels of destiny. The next weapon handed to you would be God's very righteousness. You must understand that these weapons are not just from God; they are the very divine nature of God placed within you. We know that God cannot sin because He is the complete example of righteousness. Therefore, the use of righteousness in your life would always enable you to avoid a sin fall. No demonic lion could get you off track concerning God's purpose for your life, and this would give God the full opportunity to finish His work in you. When you walk in righteousness, you are protected from all kinds of addictions and pains. Using this weapon makes you stronger than the past sins of your family. If you had a father who was an alcoholic, you could overcome that curse. If you had a mother who was a cocaine addict, you could overcome that addiction. In fact, with this weapon, regardless of the sins or secret indiscretions of your families, you would not have to be enslaved by them. You would be free!

Another weapon in your arsenal is that of the gospel witness. The very good news about Jesus who saved you is also a weapon designed to keep your feet in faith and established in the ways of God. With this weapon, you can rest assured that you will walk in the paths which God has chosen for you and not those chosen by what people think about you. Therefore, not only did you get saved by this gospel of Jesus Christ, but you are constantly being preserved by it. No matter what is failing around you, you are being kept by what is on the inside of you. Isn't this some powerful stuff?

As if this were not enough, God has also given you His very faith. With faith as a weapon, nothing is impossible for you. You will be able to call the angels to attention on your behalf. You would be able to move every mountain of distraction, doubt, poverty, and sickness. When this weapon is applied, every demon and Satan himself must step down and scatter from that vicinity. Faith would allow you to touch the realm where there is no darkness but only light, where there is no disease, just healing, and where there is no fear but only confidence. If you were to walk by faith, you would be able to see years into the God-appointed future for you because faith gives you supernatural sight into the realm of the physically unseen. Faith allows you the spiritual insight to pierce the veil of the secret and hidden things of God and to truly give you prophetic insight as to what is really about to come to the world around you. With this weapon, you would be able to better guard your life through the capability to visualize and speak the mind of God concerning your life.

After faith, God grants you the weapon of an imprinted salvation. Therefore, the salvation of God, into which you have entered, has become your mark of protection against demons. When they see this mark, they know that they cannot just launch any kind of attack against you, unless you are living in a state of constant sin after being marked as God's very own. The mark of salvation also protects your mind from the inner words of Satan and demons by helping you recognize what words are dangerous to your full faith development and giving you every opportunity to cast them out of your mind. It also helps you to want to live in holiness by constantly reminding you that you have been marked by God for His pure use. This reminder is very vital to us as we all have to be reminded from time to time that we have been chosen by God for good works and not evil works or intentions. Thank God for His mark of salvation upon us!

Then, last but not least, God has; extended to you the Word. God has spoken much of what He wished to say to us in the Bible so that we could become familiar with Him speaking future words of life and victory to us. In fact, every word from God is so life-transforming and satanically crippling, that it has the power to withstand any demonic attack. God's Words are so powerful that He made the earth and all life with them, and He governs all life, human or demonic, with them. When we, who are born of the Holy Spirit and baptized into the power of the Holy Spirit, use God's words correctly, we will bring down demonic strongholds, tear down ungodly foundations, break generational demonic ties, destroy sickness and disease, and cause sinners to fall to their sinful knees before the only God who can save them. In order for us to use this necessary weapon, we must first believe that every word from God is law and cannot ever fail when applied to any situation by faith.

I believe that at this juncture in your reading, you are probably ready to go out and kick every demon's backside! Well, I have to tell you that this would probably be the time to do it. If you have reached this page in this book, you have come to the end of this God-breathed revelation for your advancement on behalf of His kingdom. You must now prepare yourself, by the leading of the Holy Ghost, to take all of this truth and make it real within your life. I believe that if you were to do this, you would bring so many others to the place of God's destiny for them. Then, they would be able to overcome all kinds of satanic sabotage designed to hinder and destroy their very existence. So I say to you, arise! Wake up! This is your time to fight and defeat sabotage and all its many, manifested faces! In Jesus Christ and by His Holy Spirit, you will stand as the spirit of sabotage falls! My prayer is that God will move you from sabotage to triumph! May God richly bless all of you, His faithful soldiers!

ABOUT THE AUTHOR

APOSTLE KEVIN A. Johnson is a born-again worshipper of God. He is a native of the Bahamas and is the son of the late Samuel Johnson and Ms. Maud Dorcas Stubbs. Apostle Johnson is married to the former Terrah L. Rolle, and together they have been blessed with five beautiful and anointed children-Zoe, Rachel, Sarah, Benjamin, and David. Apostle Johnson lives in Nashville, Tennessee and is the senior apostle and president of Breathe Again Ministries. He and his wife are the God-appointed leaders of this local and international conference-style ministry. Apostle Johnson believes that God, by His Holy Spirit, has given spiritual gifts and physical talents to His people of faith. However, it is the responsibility of these people of faith to use His gifts and talents for the express purpose of promoting the gospel of Jesus Christ, strengthening the Church, and impacting the sinful world with the miraculous power of God. According to Apostle Johnson, these spiritual gifts and physical talents should not be used for the promotion of human egos nor for making God's servants into objects of worship. His spiritual philosophy can be summed up in this simple but powerful statement: "In order for any life to have a good end, it must be lived by and through the power and presence of the Holy Spirit!"

Should you wish to reach Apostle Kevin A. Johnson for special prayer, counseling, conferences, or revivals, please feel free to contact him at (615) 916-9479 (mobile) or email him at apostlekaj@yahoo.com or ale18@tmo.blackberry.net.